Howl of the Wolf

Howl of the Wolf:

North Carolina State University Students Call Out for Social Change

By

Rupert W. Nacoste, Ph.D.

ISBN 978-1-300-05775-8

"How lonely is the night without the howl of a wolf."

Unknown

Foreword

Like everywhere else in America, students at North Carolina State University (NCSU) are trying to understand and manage neo-diversity. That's what I have been observing and teaching since 2005.

I grew up in the Jim Crow South; that time of legal racial segregation. But now, we no longer live in a society where our racial contacts are controlled and restricted by law. Nowadays, every day, each of us has some occasion to interact with a person from another racial, ethnic or gender group. And those persons come from multiple racial, ethnic and gender groups. So, today our interpersonal encounters with race are not black and white, but neo-diverse. That is why I say today diversity in black and white is dead. Long live neo-diversity.

Fast; this has come upon us very fast. Rapid social change has put each of us in situations where we have to interact with people on an equal footing, but with people who do not look like and sometimes do not even sound like us. That is neo-diversity, and that neo-diversity creates social uncertainty about how to interact with people.

I have seen that uncertainty here at NCSU. So I created a course to help students figure out what's going on. In that course students write about their interpersonal encounters with neo-diversity, and then at the end of the course they write about their new understanding. In developing a new understanding, many write with a powerful, fresh motivation to work for a positive change in the neo-diverse environment of the NCSU campus, and of America. They almost scream it out in their papers.

In this little book, I offer to the NCSU campus the voices of those students.

Hear them.
Listen to the howl of the wolf.
Professor Rupert W. Nacoste
August, 2012

Chapter 1

Who Are the We at NCSU?

fags burn... Die...

October 17, 2011. Thick, black and bold. Those words were spray painted on the front of North Carolina State University's Gay, Lesbian, Bi-sexual, Transgender (GLBT) Center. At North Carolina State University (NCSU), it appears that some believe that gay and lesbian students have no right to life. The graffiti on the front of our GLBT Center told some of the Wolfpack to "die."

On diversity and other issues on our campus, I have the long view. Since my time in the U.S. Navy (1972-1976) I have worked on diversity issues. Part of that work has been as an activist, and part of it has been as a scholar here at NCSU when I came onto the faculty in 1988.

In fact for two years (2000-2002) I served as NCSU's first Vice Provost for Diversity and African American Affairs. Having that long and experienced a view, my eyes have seen the evolution of diversity issues in America. On this campus I have seen intolerance, indifference, fear and loathing for diversity. But I have also seen our students work to accept, embrace and celebrate our campus diversity.

Many NCSU students know about me and my work. Maybe that's why so many of our student groups invite me to

1

give talks about diversity. Fall 2011, I gave a presentation to students in our University's Honors Village. It was one of those laid back, get-to-know-the-professor kind of gatherings.

That day in the Honors Village my job was to share my history as a research scientist with the students. To do that, I had to walk them through my life, starting from my Navy experience. You see, it was in the Navy that my personal and scholarly interest in race relations and diversity really came to life.

To bring that up to date, I talked to the students about my creation and teaching of my Interpersonal Relationships and Race course. I let the students know that the reason I created the course in 2006 was because I could see that something new was happening in America and on our campus. Diversity had changed. When I started working on diversity issues in the U.S. Navy in 1974, diversity was all about black-white relations. But diversity in black and white is dead. To the students I said "… long live neo-diversity."

Neo-diversity[1] is what we live with today; a time and circumstance when, for all of us, contact with people who do not look like us happens every day, and is unavoidable. Around 2004, I began to notice that many students on our campus were having trouble adjusting to our neo-diverse America. Not so much because of prejudice and bigotry, but because of uncertainty and anxiety about how to interact. Today's 21st century struggle is interpersonal and is captured by the question that people carry with them everywhere: "Who are the 'we' and who are among the 'they?'"[2]

Whites feel uncertainty when interacting with non-whites; blacks feel uncertainty when interacting with whites and other

---

[1] Nacoste, R.W. (2006). What rough beast: Intergroup tensions in the age of neo-diversity. Forum On Public Policy, 2 (2006): 556-569.
[2] Appadurai, Arjun. Fear of Small Numbers. (2006) Durham, NC: Duke University Press.

non-blacks. There are no innocent. We are all being stalked by our uncertainty; that neo-diversity anxiety. How should I interact? Should I say something? What should I say? How should I say it? Damn, what are the rules? That anxiety means that as a nation we are a people who live in a time of interracial transition, anxiety and tension. In interracial interactions, that is why some feel jittery. But the prologue of the science fiction TV show Torchwood is right.

"The 21st century is when everything changes. You have to be ready."

So in 2006 I created a course to get students ready. I designed my course to give students a forum in which to explore and understand how another person's race, ethnicity, religion, gender or sexual orientation can create anxiety and uncertainty about how to interact with that person. In addition to just understanding what is going on, the course shows students the ways in which they can improve their interpersonal-intergroup interactions.

Every time I teach the course, my students show their hunger to understand. On the second day of class, I ask them why they signed up for a course with the title "Interpersonal Relationships and Race." I ask what they have come to the class hoping we will talk about. They answer:

What are the best ways to approach discussions about race?
What are the positives and negatives of "not seeing race"?
Why and how do interaction styles change when people interact with people of other groups?
How should you interact with people who are displaying intolerance?
Why are some people so opposed to romantic interracial relationships?

*What is going on with generational gaps (why does my
grandfather/grandmother have more difficulty accepting
those of other races?)*
What are the issues of growing up in an interracial family?
*How do you diffuse/react to a situation that becomes
racially charged?*
*What are some ways to help others in your group
open their minds?*
*Why are some things OK within a group but not
outside the group?*
How should we answer children's questions about race?
*How do stereotypes work within a group (light
skin vs. darker)?*
*How can associations with Christianity and
racism/bigotry coincide?*
*Why do people say "He is the whitest black
person I know"?*
*How should you react when someone's behavior
confirms a stereotype?*

When I ask them, "…why are first-time interracial
encounters difficult to manage?" my students admit their
intergroup anxiety. They say:

It's a new experience.
Fearing the unknown.
Fear of offending.

In my presentation in the Honors Village, I described my
course to the students who came to listen. I made it clear that
there are no innocent. Everyone is struggling with the neo-
diversity question, "…who are the 'we' and who are among the
'they.'" But, I said, keep in mind everybody at NCSU is a "we."
Everybody here is Wolfpack. On that Friday afternoon, I had

fun with those students, and then I went home. That evening I got an email from one of those students. She wrote:

> *"I just wanted to thank you for sharing your experience and perspective on diversity with us at the Honors Colloquium. I attended a large public high school, where the bottom line was 'diversity is good.' However, I've often asked myself: What is diversity, exactly? Why is it such a big issue? Your perspective and the whole idea of a "we" has given me a much deeper understanding of diversity and why it's so difficult, especially for Americans, to find peace with it. It's not necessarily about putting the Chinese, African Americans, Caucasians, etc. into a room together -- it's about developing understanding and acceptance. I think this interpersonal connection is a societal necessity that a lot of people do not understand and therefore do not strive for."*

Turns out, we continue to do a lousy job of teaching young people about diversity and why it is important in America. We continue to offer only sound bites like "diversity is good." Having been given no substance, young people leave high school confused about diversity. And too often young people like you end up at colleges and universities where that confusion continues, because there too you get nothing but "diversity is good" sound bites.

But what the email from that young woman tells me is that students at N.C. State want substance. you are looking for a real understanding. That email and what I see happen to students in my class tells me something important: Once students come to understand that the real challenge today is interpersonal, they feel better, calmer, and more prepared to live, go to class, and eventually work within our neo-diverse communities.

But all is not yet well. Every now and then we are reminded of that.

fags burn... Die...

That is the graffiti that was spray painted on the front of the *university property* that is our GLBT center. Clearly some of our students forget, or do not want to accept that the first words of the preamble of the Declaration of Independence are:

"We hold these truths to be self-evident, that all men are created equal. That they are endowed by their creator with certain inalienable rights; among these are life, liberty and the pursuit of happiness."

Self-evident. Meaning it's so obvious that there's no need for a discussion or explanation.

Regarding our preamble, former U.S. Secretary of State General Colin Powell said:

"This beautiful statement was not the reality of 1776, but it set forth the dream that we would strive to make a reality ... Governments belong to the people and exist to secure the rights endowed to every citizen."

Yes, for a long time America said that these words did not apply to someone with my dark skin color. Slavery, and then racial segregation were evidence of no right to liberty, no right to choose where to live or go to school, and no right to vote until 1965. No right to choose who to marry, no right to that pursuit of happiness until 1967.

Born in 1951, I grew up in the segregated-by-law Jim Crow South. That racial segregation did something very important. Racial segregation made it clear who was part of "we" and who was part of "they." By law, the "we" had places to go that the "they" could not; *by law*. With those immoral laws gone, we now live in a time when interacting with someone who does not look like us is unavoidable. What's left now, our greatest challenge, is learning to interact with each other as equals. Now we live in a time when contact with people who do not look like or even sound like us is unavoidable. So we struggle with the neo-diversity question, who are the "we" and who are among the "they."

By being admitted to the university, everybody on our campus is an NCSU "we," and everyone in any class is a part of the Wolfpack. Our challenge today is to accept and live in that reality. Have no doubt that neo-diversity anxiety is causing some of us to want to keep some Wolfpack students in the category of "they" and "them." We have seen that anxiety in negative racial and anti-gay and lesbian graffiti on our campus. Yet some of us understand that the hate of a group expressed in graffiti is really an attack on students of all sexual orientations, racial and religious stripes, because it shows that there is intolerance and hate on our campus. Who wants to live in a place like that? How can a person go home and proclaim their pride in being a student at a place that is hateful?

Yet we know that not everybody at NCSU accepts that this has to be a hateful place. Recently, when racial graffiti appeared in the Free Expression Tunnel, NCSU students howled in anger. Those howls came from white students, too. That is part of the neo-diversity of our campus. White students at NCSU are not all of one mind about racial matters. So yeah, some simpleton writes racial graffiti, but that does not reflect the opinion of the whole campus. Among all of our students there are different racial, moral codes, and interpersonal relationships. No surprise, then, that racial graffiti is taken as an attack on all our students because it shows that there is intolerance and hate on the campus.

When word of the racial graffiti moved across campus, the Wolf awoke. When anti-black and anti-gay graffiti was found in our "Free-Expression" tunnel, white students were upset; so too straight students. Not only that, but with Latina-Hispanic, white, African-American, male, Arab, straight, Hindu, female, Asian, brown, and other students as equal partners, many students started organizing themselves against that foolishness.

So on our campus, we do react when intolerance and hate goes public in the Free Expression Tunnel or there is some specific intolerant attack aimed at one of our student groups. I was very proud of our campus outcry against the hate aimed at our Gay, Lesbian, Bi-sexual, Trans-gendered students. Very proud.

Yet given the long view, I know that not that long ago there would not have been any such outcry. So something new was happening. A new awareness and acceptance of neo-diversity was growing. It was akin to what I see in students who take my "Interpersonal Relationships and Race" course. Each semester, as the course progresses, my students begin to develop a new awareness and a new understanding of the neo-diversity dynamics of America. And when it sinks in, when my students get it, they howl.

Oh how they howl, demanding to know why it has taken so long for our educational system to tell them the truth. In their papers they howl about being able to see dynamics around them that, before, they did not know to even look for. And they want others to know. So my students howl the truth of their new understanding, and their new willingness to object to, stand against, the forces of hate they see on our campus.

But before they howl, they growl.

Chapter 2:

No Innocent

On the first day of my "Interpersonal Relationships and Race" class, I proclaim, "When it comes to racial matters in America, there are no innocent."

Hear the growl of the Wolfpack:

> *When I first heard Dr. Nacoste confidently state at the beginning of the semester, "There are no innocent," my first thought was: "What is he talking about? Of course there are!" Being aware of the class we were in, I assumed he was referring to people who are bigoted, stubborn, stereotypical, or those who say racial slurs. "Of course there are innocent," I told myself again. Not everyone believes in white supremacy...! As Dr. Nacoste continued to claim that "there are no innocent..." I struggled to accept it, yet decided to go along with "his belief" with the notion that I myself was an outlier.*

When it comes to racial matters in America, there are no innocent.

I tell this truth because I know you came to NCSU with certain hopes and expectations. Everyone does as they move into a new situation, a new phase of life. Especially when coming out of high school, you looked forward to the new

9

situation. You hoped, you imagined how well it would go. You imagined what your new freedoms would feel like, would look like. But then the reality of things you had not imagined came; the realities of the actual features of the situation in which you had put yourself.

Thirty-five thousand students walking and talking on the campus of North Carolina State University is part of that reality. Thirty-five thousand. Among those 35,000 there are yellow, white, black and brown students. There are Christian, Jewish, Muslim, Atheist, Hindu, Buddhist students.

"Hey, no problem. I'm not prejudiced. I can interact with anybody."

Then you found yourself in one of those new, exciting situations. And you wanted to be liked. You wanted to be cool. Here's what one member of the Wolfpack admitted:

> *"Whenever I meet someone of a different race or just slightly different than me, I freak out. I say something at [an interpersonal] level in which I am NOT participating in with this person. I think the best example I have of that is... when I was meeting friends of friends at a sporting event. Already nervous from hoping they thought I was "cool", I was introduced to one of the guys and said,*
> *'What's up, homie?'*
> *Wait, what?*
> *Let me explain: I am a white girl with blonde hair and the person I just referred to as '...homie' was a 6 foot muscular build black boy.*
> *HOMIE?!*
> *I'm sitting here shaking my head right now just thinking about it. Thankfully, he didn't act very offended, he probably just thought I was trying too hard."*

When it comes to racial matters in America, there are no innocent.

You have seen things. You have done things. But in the seeing and the doing, you have not understood. Yet, that does not make you innocent. So many of your mistakes have happened because you sometimes let your hopes ("I'm cool, right?") and dreams for this new life override some of the realities that must be faced. Not innocent... but sometimes, certainly naïve. So yes, you and my students have seen things. For sure I know this about my students because I ask them to write about their most intense, interracial, intergroup experience... and they do.

So homie, what kind of experiences do they write about? Their assignment is to answer this question: *What is the most intense (odd, angry, happy, curious, threatening, challenging) interracial (intergroup)* **two-person** *interaction you have experienced?*

My students write about their most intense (odd, exciting, tense, happy, hurtful, disturbing) interpersonal-intergroup experience. Experiences that show how their innocence was lost.

When it comes to an interaction that was curious and disturbing, one student wrote:

> *A month ago I went to my girlfriend's parents' house in Charlotte for the Labor Day weekend. Her family are very involved at their church, and they invited me to come help out with Sunday school. It was there – Sunday school, of all places – that I experienced the most curious interracial dyadic interaction of my life. Here's what happened:*
>
> *The lesson of the day was not to be quick to judge. We had the kids play a game where we told them to draw something and then they would draw it and the rest of the kids had to try and guess what was drawn.*

Every time the kids would guess wrong, we would step in and note, "See? Judging quickly doesn't work!"

The first kid – the youngest of the group, aged five – drew Michael Jordan, and then the rest of the kids – mostly six or seven – guessed correctly who it was relatively quickly. After three or four more kids had gone up, a boy named Cameron came up to draw his. I whispered into his ear who he was supposed to draw. He went to the back of the room, took a couple of minutes to paint his masterpiece, then returned and held his picture up for everyone to see.

The picture he had drawn was that of a gun-toting terrorist. The man had a turban, a cigarette in his mouth, and a machine gun spewing bullets in each hand. Immediately my girlfriend took the page from Cameron and said, "Cameron, that's inappropriate!"

I went up to Cameron and asked, "Cameron, why did you draw that?"

Cameron, replied, "I saw the name and I thought he was a terrorist!"

I told Cameron immediately, "Cameron, that is the most common name in the world. Not everyone with that name is a terrorist. You can't assume what people are from their name."

Cameron nodded and ran off. My girlfriend approached me and asked, "Who was he supposed to draw?"

I looked at her and said, "Muhammad Ali".

Yikes! Oh no…

When I was a teenager, when we heard the name Muhammad Ali we immediately thought and often said out loud, "Float like a butterfly, sting like a bee." Now apparently it's, "Float like a butterfly, sting like a terrorist." How did we get here from there?

And no, this experience did not happen on campus. But it did happen in the life of one of the Wolfpack, and we bring all our experiences to campus with us. One student wrote:

> *I personally am reminded of Jim Crow [government mandated racial segregation] each and every time I visit home. I struggle with it continuously and it makes me upset and angry!!*
>
> *My grandparents, mother, aunts, uncles, great aunts, great uncles, my whole family grew up during this time inside or around Oxford, mostly in Henderson. I am constantly faced with opposing views with my family. Like I mentioned, they are from that particular time and still have very strong opinions and emotions.*
>
> *When I moved into a new apartment, I was faced with something that really hurt me. I moved into Wolf Village, the on-campus apartments here at NC State. I knew one of my roommates coming into this new apartment because we signed up together. Brittany, a black female, is a close friend of mine so we decided to move in together. However, we did not find two other females to move in with us. So, we were randomly assigned other roommates. My aunt helped me move in and when she noticed that all three of my roommates were black she said things like:*
>
> *"Are you going to be able to live with three black girls?"*
>
> *"You can request a new room assignment, right?"*
>
> *Even now when I go home she questions me about my living with three black girls and still asks if I have moved into a new apartment with different girls. As a 20 year old white female, this infuriates me and makes me very upset! When will they change their ways? It's very saddening to me.*

This young woman came to our campus with social pressures against interacting with racial-others. Some of you came with social pressures against interacting with gays and lesbians. Some of you came with social pressures against interacting with religious-others. No matter, however, because on our campus you don't have a choice. That social-other is your classmate or at least is a fellow student. That social-other is Wolfpack. How, then, will you and have you dealt with those social tensions you brought with you to campus?

****

Although my course is called "Interpersonal Relationships and Race," the course is really about any of our interactions that involve two people from different groups. It is these intergroup interactions where there is a lot of neo-diversity anxiety and hostility. That's true even when it comes to females and males. About an on-campus challenging interaction, a female student wrote:

> *I am intramural chair for my sorority and part of my job description is to handle the logistical part of the sports such as creating the teams and speaking with the referees prior to each game. On one particular night, we had a co-rec flag football game in which we paired with a fraternity. I organized our team so I was technically the captain.*
>
> *At the start of each game, the two captains from each team meet in the center of the field to review sportsmanship rules, determine who gets the ball first, and answer any last minute questions. Prior to this particular game, I had never once felt discriminated against for being the only girl captain of a co-rec team; in fact, I enjoyed it because I usually got to chosen to play 'odd-or-even' (the game used to determine possession).*

14

As I walked out to the middle of the field, the other captain approached me, stuck out his hand and introduced himself. Together, we continued on towards the referees. The head ref looked at the male captain and asked if he understood the consequences of playing with unsportsmanlike conduct. I answered 'yes' even though he wasn't directly asking me. As he continued to look at the male captain, he asked if he understood all the rules. Again, I shook my head yes. Looking at the male captain, he once again asked him to choose odd or even. Not once did he attempt to include me in the interaction or make eye contact with me.

As the rules have it, one captain decides possession of the ball and the other captain decides the direction of play. Finally, I thought, it was time when the ref was going to be forced to interact with me. For the first time I walked onto the field, the ref angled his head towards me. His body remained facing the male captain and his eyes were glued to the trees above my head. He, for the first time in three minutes, addressed me directly. I answered but got no response as he returned to face the male captain. The ref dismissed us, and when I say this, I mean the ref said 'good luck' while still looking at the male captain.

As I walked back to my team, I was fuming. I had never before been stereotyped to that degree, let alone, from someone with authority in the area. We won the game, I played well and proved to the ref that just because I was girl, that did not mean I was incompetent or incapable of playing football. At the end of the game, captains are supposed to sign the score sheet. The ref found the male captain for him to sign, but found a boy from my team to sign our sheet. I couldn't help but laugh as I walked off the field.

A young man, a student on our campus with the responsibility of being a referee, could not look a team captain in the eye because that captain was female. He treated her as if she were not a member of the Wolfpack; in fact he treated her as if she was invisible. That's not how it's supposed to go. After all, woman or man, here at NCSU we are all Wolfpack.

"You know too much," my mother used to say to warn me, to make me realize that I was acting as if I knew all I needed to know when I knew very little. Not to excuse intergroup arrogance, but sometimes people just assume too much. That comes from thinking you know enough, if not about how the world works but at least what you can say in the group of people you are interacting with. You know too much. About that, one student wrote:

> *If you were to learn my name before seeing my face, you might be a little confused. While a name like "Chavez" definitely looks Hispanic, my pale skin, light brown curly hair, and blue eyes lead most people to simply classify me as "White." Although sometimes it takes a little convincing to get people to believe that I am actually Hispanic, my friends and closer acquaintances have all come to know and respect that part about me. The thing is, you cannot always depend on other people to refrain from relying on their visual assumptions.*
>
> *We were all in high school, just hanging out on a Saturday night like usual. Some of my friends had brought some of their friends along, which gave me the opportunity to get to know them in a group conversation. One of the "new" guys was talking about the work that his family was having done on their house. I think they were putting on a new roof or something. He went into detail about his experience with the roofers in the previous week.*

"They are all these dang Mexicans! They are out there hammering away at our house at 8 in the morning and just speaking Spanish all day. Who knows, they are probably all illegal anyways. Maybe I should go out tomorrow and start talking to them. 'Ho-la. Co-mo e-stas? Me gus-ta tacos.'"

My friends, all being well aware of my ethnicity and of my lack of tolerance for ignorance, froze and just looked at me. They had no idea what to say to the guy and were all on edge to see how I would react.

I considered the fact that we all come from a small town and therefore are exposed to small town, narrow-minded mentality quite often. I figured I would give him the benefit of the doubt and let him redeem himself. Completely oblivious to his racial slurs and the increased tension in the room, the new guy looked around to all of us and asked,

"What do you think? My Spanish is pretty good right? I mean, good enough to just talk to them."

Again, silence and discomfort.

"Yea it's great... as long as all the workers are under the age of three. But I doubt they are and after hearing my dad's family, the Chavezes, speak fluent Spanish, I would say you have some practice to do before you try to dive into any serious conversation."

The kid just looked at me and at everyone else, not really sure how to take what I said.

"On second thought, you might just want to leave them alone. I mean, since they are illegal they would probably prefer to get in and get out right?"

I could see all of my friends suppress snickers and "ohhhs!" while the other guy still stumbled around in his own mind trying to interpret everything. Having said what I needed to say and proving the point that I needed to prove, I got up from my seat on the arm of

17

the couch and went outside to talk to some of my other friends in perfectly fluent English.

Are we having fun yet?

That was high school. But trust me, all of you have brought some high school ways of thinking and behaving with you to NCSU. For example, one student wrote:

I am Mexican American but most people do not know this because I do not look like I am and I do not speak Spanish. I never really tell people either because how awkward is it to say "Hi, I am Karissa and I am half Mexican?" I only tell people when they either ask or have said something about Mexicans and I willingly announce it. Because of this, I have been in some interesting interactions.

One interaction in particular, I was with a close friend of mine, who is white, and we were going to meet up for dinner with a couple more of her friends, who are also white, that I had met before but did not know enough to be friends. When we got to dinner we were all talking and getting along fine. At one point during dinner, my friend and one of the other girls needed to go to the bathroom so they excused themselves. The girl I was left with at the table continued to talk to me and we were laughing and joking around. The next thing I know a Mexican family of eight walks in and this girl says, "I wonder if they all came in the same car? You know how those Mexicans pack into a car like sardines."

Immediately, I became a little standoffish. I did not get that upset initially because I am used to hearing these slurs all the time and it was not directed at me. As soon as I told her my ethnicity she got this look on her face, stopped making eye contact with me and got quiet

18

for a few seconds. I just sat there and kept looking around for my friend to come back so at least some of the awkwardness would be relieved.

All of the sudden she looks at me and says, "Sorry, but I cannot be friends with a wetback."

My mouth immediately dropped and I literally had no words. I was so angry that I got up from the table, went to the bathroom to find my friend and told her we had to leave right away. I knew I needed to leave because if I would have said anything to her, it would not have been a good situation. My friend went back to the table and said we had to leave, but I refused to go back to the table so I just made my way to the door. As I was walking through the restaurant, the girl and I made eye contact and before I realized, I rolled my eyes at her. I am pretty sure that is the last time I ever spoke to her.

Neo-diversity anxiety is a hell of thing. Whites feel uncertainty when interacting with non-whites. Blacks feel uncertainty when interacting with whites and other non-blacks. There are no innocent.

How should I interact? Should I say something? What should I say? How should I say it? Damn, what are the rules? That anxiety does not have to turn a person into a bigot. But it can. Rather than try to learn to interact across an intergroup dimension, some people just give up: I can't do this, I can't interact with you. I can't be your friend. And to make that very clear, I call you a name: wetback. That is a conscious decision.

There are no innocent.

****

No matter what, no matter the social pressures against interacting with "others" that we bring to a new situation, everyone has to interact with somebody. No woman or man is an island. No one should live in a closet. No one can survive by trying to live life in a closet. We are, by design, social.

And social interaction is a powerful force. The more we interact with a person, the more comfortable we become. Sometimes that is dangerous. Why? Because that comfort may make us feel that we can say things to a person as if we were still at home, without thinking about the demeaning power of our words. One student wrote:

> *I am Palestinian-American and make no attempt at hiding that. All of my friends are well aware of my ethnicity and the attacks and prejudices middle-easterners are faced with.*
>
> *The situation played out like this... My white-female roommate had just gotten home from visiting her boyfriend in Chicago. It was her first time flying alone and I knew she had been nervous. Upon her arrival back at the apartment, we were both sitting on the couch watching TV and talking. I was asking her about her trip and how her flights went. Everything was going great until she paused, hesitating a little bit and said, "Whenever you fly, do you ever look around at the people you are flying with and freak out when you see terrorists?"*
>
> *Terrorists. She said terrorists. I am fairly certain my jaw hit the ground.*
>
> *She then followed that up by saying it doesn't even have to be on a plane. I was trying to remain calm and responded with, "What do you mean?" She replied back with, "You know, Arabs." Except she didn't even say Arabs, she said "A-rabs."*
>
> *AS IF the terrorist comment wasn't bad enough, she added insult to injury by saying, "A-rabs," one of my absolute biggest pet peeves. I did not know what to*

20

say or how to react. I mean, this was one of my best friends and someone I live with. The last thing I wanted was to have tension or be fighting with someone I reside with. In an attempt to not say things I would later regret, I simply got up and went to my room, but before shutting my door, I said, "No, I never do that, Emily."

The way in which I responded to the situation was so horribly wrong and shameful. I should have confronted her right then and there. I should have expressed to her how disappointed and pissed off I was that she had just indirectly referred to my family and I as terrorists. I should have given her a history lesson and then signed her up for Dr. Nacoste's class.

Is anybody home?

Turns out that once you leave home you need to spend time learning how to adapt to and interact in new situations. Not everybody you interact with, even someone you interact with every day, is to be treated as if they come from your home. At NCSU we all encounter and interact with a neo-diversity of people. For the mature person, that should mean you know better than to just say the first thing that pops in your head.

One student wrote:

The night that I am about to recount is one that I will never forget, now a memory of a night that not only impacted my life but several other people's lives as well.

It all started when myself and a couple of my other fraternity members were hanging out, drinking a few casual beers at my house on a Friday night. The situation was nothing new, I was used to hanging out with my fraternity members on weekends, however this night was slightly different than the rest because we had just initiated some new members into the chapter, and it was these young initiates first time out as "brothers."

One of the new initiates was a black male, the only black man to enter our chapter in quite a while. As we all sat drinking our beers and steadily getting a bit "tipsy," everything was going fine and everyone seemed to be having a great time enjoying each others' company.

Once again, there was nothing unusual about this night. However, that was all about to change indefinitely. As I sat, having a conversation with the new black initiate to our fraternity, I remember seeing his eyes light up as we both heard in the background someone in the room who had in a joking manner chanted "white power."

What inspired this person, who I formerly regarded as a friend, to shout such a thing is to this day beyond my comprehension. It was anything but a joke to the black man in the room, whom I had been talking to and had now stopped mid-sentence to address what had been heard. The room fell silent, as our black initiate repeatedly asked if he had heard correctly.

I was in shock. I had never expected anyone in my fraternity, nonetheless, my group of friends to ever make such a comment and wanted to somehow make it right with the man who I still regarded as a new friend. As rapidly as the interaction had begun, it ended, with the black man exiting my house, never seeking to have contact with our fraternity again.

Soon, I too chose the same fate.

Intergroup interactions can get out of hand when students keep trying to live out the attitudes about a group that they grew up with. Expressing those beliefs is your right as long as you are willing to live out the consequences. Remember the other person has the same rights as you.

So expressing those beliefs, trying to live them out, can lead to intense interactions. One student wrote:

> *It was my freshman year of college. My ex-boyfriend, his friend, and I were riding together from our hometown to an NC State football game on a Saturday afternoon. I really didn't want to ride with him in the first place, but I didn't have a car, and I had no way of getting back to Raleigh for the Saturday game without his help. I was planning on meeting up with other friends when we got to Raleigh and going to the game with them.*
>
> *My ex-boyfriend and I had broken up after a very short relationship before I left for college because I thought he was small-minded and judgmental. Often when we were out together, he would make comments about people as they passed by. He claimed to hate Yankees, black people, Canadians, jocks, and anyone from Asia.*
>
> *That's why he was my last resort for a ride to the football game. As we drove, he and his friend were talking about a black man that they had seen at a gas station. They were talking about how he probably stole the food he was coming out of the gas station with.*
>
> *Then they switched the topic to women. My ex-boyfriend made a comment that the only thing women were good for was oral sex, and his friend added "and making sandwiches." At that point, I said "pull over." He started saying that I was being 'too sensitive.' I said again, "pull over."*
>
> *He pulled over on the side of 401 North, and I got out of the car. He squealed his tires as he took off, and left me on the side of the road. A friend picked me up 20 minutes later. I ended up missing the first part of the game, but standing up for myself was more important to me than football.*

Now that was risky. Wow! That is really standing up for yourself. Risky yes; but to stand up for what is right takes risk.

By the way, being from a group that is usually the target of slurs does not mean you are innocent. Students from all groups have to deal with neo-diversity anxiety and finding appropriate ways to communicate in intergroup situations. One student wrote:

One of the most awkward interracial dyadic interactions I have experienced was at the beginning of the 2011 Fall semester. I had already moved into the dorm due to the fact that Community Assistants have to work while other students are moving in.

After a few days of having the room to myself, my roommate moved in and we were getting the feel for one another. On one particular day, we are both sitting on our beds, which are on opposite sides of the small dorm room, talking about random things. Some of the things we are talking about are, what each other's major are, what part of North Carolina we're from, etc.

At this point in the conversation she is telling me who her friends are and trying to figure out if I knew them or not, being that I'm a CA and I'm familiar with a lot of the residents in this dormitory. She starts describing one particular friend by saying "she's short, wears glasses, and she's (she pauses for a moment) colored."

The only thing running through my mind at this point is race riots in the streets of Birmingham, Alabama, Martin Luther King Jr., every civil rights landmark from the 60s, and I feel myself get angry. To avoid cursing her out, I cut her off mid-sentence and say with authority, "She's black." To which she responds <u>as a Mexican-American</u>, "She's black, *whatever," and rolls her eyes, as if me correcting her was pointless.*

Whatever? Whatever? I felt my anger rising for the simple fact that with that whatever I felt that she was sweeping my race's history under the rug, as if it didn't matter, so I stopped listening to her.

I think she noticed this and she finally stopped talking. Talk about awkward. After that demeaning conversation, we never really talked again and it's always been awkward when she and I are in the room alone. Sad, I know.

Look, these interactions happen because as a nation we have tried to quickly get past the past. But the past is still here. Unfortunately, you young people bear the brunt of our nation not teaching you about the deep (racial, gender, ethnic, religious) hurts in our nation's history. And so you make mistakes. When you do, at the moment you do, you often don't know what is going on. One student wrote:

I was about 10 years old. I was at a friend's house. I knew Sam from school. We were playing and then we would have dinner. When it was dinner time we all came and sat at the table. His family was very nice and they said a prayer while holding hands before we started eating. When we finished bowing our heads, I looked up to see what we were having for dinner. It was a bowl of chili with meat and beans, shredded cheddar cheese, sour cream, tortillas, and ground beef.

Excitedly, I shouted "Oh, I love this. We call it spick food." Immediately the parents froze and everyone seemed to get tense.

I looked around, not understanding the social clues. The father leaned toward me and said something like "We don't use that kind of language here."

I had no idea what could have offended them. I was so confused. My naivety had made me look so ignorant and looking back I am very embarrassed at the interaction.

Back then I was simple-minded and innocent, that's how I know I did not mean anything malicious by it. I was just repeating what I was taught. The only reason I knew that offensive word was because of my family. They, being ignorant as well, had heard it and started calling Mexican/Spanish foods "spick" food.

Years later my mother told me that she was embarrassed too. She said she did not even know that was a racial slur until that event woke her up. That experience made me "racially aware," showed me the importance of race relations, and instilled in me the urge to be sensitive to other's feelings, especially in social settings. My relationship with Sam was never quite the same. I do not think I went to his house for dinner again.

"Spick food." Yes, same as wet-back, the word spick is a racial slur. Still, he was innocent. He was a 10-year-old just repeating what he learned in his home. But we don't have any 10-year-old students at NCSU. Even understanding that not every student who comes to our campus is worldly, in this age of information overflow and saturation, saying "I didn't know" just won't cut it.

You have seen things. You have done things. But in the seeing and the doing, you have not understood. Yet, that does not make you innocent. So many of your mistakes have happened because you sometimes let your hopes ("I'm cool, right?") and dreams for this new life override some of the realities that must be faced. Not innocent... but sometimes, certainly, arrogant in your unwillingness to face the truth about your mistakes.

Here's the problem.

You know too much. Too many of you think you know enough about this race stuff, about these intergroup matters. But as these stories from other NCSU students make clear, you don't. Not just about race, but ethnicity and even gender.

And the truth is, you have been duped. You have been misled by not being taught the whole truth. But now you are adults, or so you say. That means that now it's time for you to face up to the reality that has caused some of you to make "innocent" mistakes, and some of you to behave as bigots.

I help my students with that.

I show them the blood.

Chapter 3:

Blood

"I am shocked to find out about the riots in Wilmington! Why have I never heard of such a thing when I LIVE in North Carolina? Why has it been kept hush from North Carolina history? I am completely appalled."

A.B. Junior, NCSU

Going from believing you know something, to finding out you knew nothing, will make you growl with hunger and anger. One student wrote:

"As the semester continued, concepts were introduced and stories/experiences were shared to exemplify and personalize every person's lack of innocence. I soon began to comprehend the fact that there truly are no innocent, not even me. Continuing to discuss concepts and ideas, connections were soon made. It came to my knowledge that anxiety... plays a large role in the bold statement: 'There are no innocent.' Beyond this however, I began to accept, know, and internalize everyone's lack of innocence, including my own."

Look, I understand that when your generation of NCSU students feels racial tension in a particular interaction or in a social setting, you don't really know why. Your generation was not around in 1968, the year that Newsweek has dubbed "...the year that made us who we are..." (Newsweek, 2007). Your generation was not among those who were the first to begin to directly address and fight through the question, "What rights were owed to African-Americans, to women, to gays?" But you want to know, need to know, what is the source of the tension?

For instance, when on our campus a paper lynching-noose was found, black students were outraged and fearful. Yet many of their white classmates asked, "Why are *they* making such a big deal?"

Likewise when in November 2008, the morning after the election of Barack Hussein Obama as our President, racial graffiti and a racial threat against our new president were found in the Free Expression Tunnel, some NCSU students again asked, "...what's the big deal?" In November 2009 it happened again. Then, November 2011, more racial and this time anti-gay graffiti was once again found in the Free Expression Tunnel. But this time something curious happened.

Wednesday, November 3, 2011. Sitting in my office at my desk checking my email, I got one from a former student who by then was an alumnus. She asked, *"...what is going on at my school?"* Immediately following that one, I got another, also from a recent NCSU-graduate. She wrote, *"I... wanted to email you to ask if you knew of the 'Blackout-Against-Racism' event on Facebook that is exploding with reactions and tensions relating to the Obama Free Expression Tunnel incident?"* Yes, it happened again. More anti-black graffiti, this time combined with anti-gay hateful sentiments. I knew nothing about this. I investigated. What I learned disturbed me. But that was about the lack of information on our campus. No word had come to the faculty. Neo-diversity anxiety had apparently caused the NCSU administration to hesitate.

Next day, Thursday, November 4, 2010, in my "Interpersonal Relationships and Race" course, I led an impromptu discussion about the new Free Expression Tunnel "Racial Graffiti."

"How many of you have heard about the recent racial graffiti in the Free Expression Tunnel?"

Only twenty-eight out of the racial, ethnic and gender mix of 60 students had heard something.

"What have you heard?"

One answer was, *"There was a picture of Obama doing indecent things and the N-word was written."*

"How did you hear?"

Students first heard about this through calls from family whose sources included the *Washington Post*, State Fans Nation, Facebook Event, *Raleigh News and Observer*. Most surprising—one grandmother had seen a report on Good Morning America and called her grandson.

That pattern made one student ask, *"...why do people outside of the university know more than the people within it?"* So what about information from our campus sources? Even by the time I conducted that Thursday in-class discussion, nothing had appeared in the *Technician* about what had happened on Tuesday night. With disgust one student said, *"...student leaders and student media outlets got an email about this incident. The university was very selective about who they shared this info with."* Whatever the email said to student leaders, the communication did not contain much information. One student said, *"...there is still a lot of confusion. Nobody wants to say or tell about what was really written in the tunnel."*

Until I gave each a copy, none of my sixty students had seen the statement Chancellor Randy Woodson had released. Dated November 2, 2010, Chancellor Woodson's statement began:

> *"Tensions tend to run high during election season and this year is no exception. Here in North Carolina all you have to do is turn on the television set to see that frustration and concern about any number of issues have worked their way into the political process at just about*

every level. There are challenges on campus as well, but as I said last summer, I believe we have an opportunity here to move NC State to new heights.

There is a renewed sense of pride on campus and I see that on the faces of the students, faculty and staff that I encounter every day. I hear it from alumni and the general public. The outpouring of good will and caring among the Wolfpack family is true and genuine.

But we still have work to do. The thoughtless act of defacing the Free Expression Tunnel with racially charged obscenities and derogatory comments directed to the GLBT community reminds us of that.

In order to achieve our goals and to prepare students for the global workplace, we must create an environment and an overall sense of global awareness on campus that encourages and embraces all forms of diversity.

Yes, it had been posted on the NCSU website, but you had to search to find it. Reading the statement, my students felt that *"...this [statement] is nothing but vague and it doesn't confront anything directly."* Reacting, my students were puzzled. *"He says a renewed sense of pride. Does he think we are proud of what just happened."* Another student said, *"The people that did this will just read this statement and laugh and feel as though they can do this again and get away with it."*

Going on, Chancellor Woodson said:

The real value of the Free Expression Tunnel is that it is an icon. It is the embodiment of free speech, a place where we can air our thoughts openly. It's a place where, to cite a recent example, design students can choose to express their appreciation for their Dean. And, it's a place where frustrations are aired even when those frustrations take on the most negative tones.

But, here's the reality: the Free Expression Tunnel is us. What we say and do there says as much about us as the clothes we wear, the ethics we live our lives by and the politics we practice. The question for us all is are we going to practice the politics of hate and destruction, or are we going to be a force for respectful dialog even where there are differences of opinion?

We must remain committed to the collective pursuit of excellence through acceptance of both individuals and ideas that may be different than our own, for these are the things that will continue to move us all forward.

Diversity makes our lives richer and gives us the chance to advance our university by encouraging a culture that values empathy, respect and equality for all. By doing this, we hope to be paving the road for a more diverse and inclusive world – both at home and abroad.

Now I could feel the anger in the classroom. Voice trembling, one student said, *"What is he talking about? I can tell you the Free-Expression Tunnel is not me... it never has represented me."* Also angry, another said, *"Chancellor's job is to speak on behalf of NCSU, but he is addressing others and not informing 'us.'"*

We have got to do better. Chancellor Woodson was right when he wrote that *"...we still have work to do."* But, I mean that the university has to better communicate with students about important neo-diversity matters. If something happens that is important enough for the Chancellor to release a statement on his portion of the NCSU website, then communication with students should be direct and timely.

Without direct communication, misinformation and rumors will spread throughout the NCSU community. Students will develop their own ideas about what has happened and what to do about it. One student said, *"If students aren't guided by the administration, they'll fill the vacuum with their own ideas of how to react."* Into that vacuum intergroup tension will rise up. *"If they're going to do a blackout, I'll wear white,"* was a statement overheard by one of my students.

Other problems will also crop up. Lack of direct communication with our student-citizens about a neo-diversity incident will lead to all kinds of interpretations of the agenda of the university. Reading the Chancellor's statement, one student said that given its tone, *"[The Chancellor's] political agenda is now called into question!"* My students were angry because as one put it, *"...we feel like children when not informed; speak to us like adults."*

Word did get around that this had made local and national TV news. What brought the national attention was the fact that some African American students had, for about an hour, blocked other students from using the Free Expression Tunnel to get to class.

Why object? "What's the big deal?" some students asked again. Even some professors wondered about the level of risks some African American students had been willing to take. Speaking with a degree of accuracy, some said, "I've seen worse graffiti on the stalls in men's bathrooms on campus, so why this big reaction to this particular racial graffiti?"

Yes we have seen worse things in bathroom stalls. So I asked myself, what are we not teaching these African American students who are so outraged as to be ready to break the law? Here the law was not unjust or immoral. The law in question had to do with physically blocking other students' access to a tunnel to their legitimate destinations on campus. Why were students willing to risk being arrested for that?

Then it occurred to me that for these African American students, like for all the other students, this is college. This is college and university life that was supposed to be the "...best time in their lives." For all of our students and college students everywhere, this time is supposed to be that time between being a child, a minor, and being a real adult (paying rent and all that). So this is supposed to be football and basketball games, parties, frivolity, while taking classes to get that degree. But now, with public, offensive, racial graffiti aimed at your group, it's not that. Damn, the real world is already here and so the dream is deferred. Sadly, probably forever.

That is why some black students were demanding something even they knew was ridiculous: a guarantee that this will never happen again; or at least while they are still a student here. Those students were angry at the loss of the college dream, at the loss of their innocence. So that's why they said, "...oh it's on..." as a threat, but an empty threat.

What happens to a dream deferred is what Langston Hughes asked:

"Does it stink like rotten meat?
Or crust and sugar over like a syrupy sweet?
Maybe it just sags like a heavy load...
Or does it explode?"

A dream deferred in the name of "...free expression." But it is a dream deferred only for students who are members of certain American groups. Is that really the point of "...free expression," or the result of completely confusing the idea of "...free expression" with the constitutional right of freedom of speech?

****

Free expression and freedom of speech are not the same thing. In America, no one has a right to total free-expression. What the constitution says is:

Congress shall make no law respecting an
establishment of religion, or prohibiting the free
exercise thereof; or abridging the freedom of speech,
or of the press; or the right of the people peaceably to

assemble, and to petition the Government for a redress of grievances.

No accident that this is in the Bill of Rights, the 1st Amendment of the U.S. Constitution. In America, freedom of speech is a right, privilege and a responsibility. The relevant part of the 1st Amendment reads:

Congress shall make no law ... abridging the freedom of speech

Freedom of speech protects citizens from *government* trying to silence a citizen's expression of ideas and claims. Freedom of speech, however, protects no citizen from rebuttal from other citizens. Freedom of speech does not protect "free expression" because free expression does not require you to identify yourself. Free expression does not even require that you stand by and represent your ideas. That's why free expression is almost always done unseen, in the shadows.

The KKK wore hoods to hide their faces, and they only rode out at night. That shows you that free expression is immature and is the dark tunnel that immature citizens live in and prefer.

Free expression, you see, allows people to hide and not have their claims challenged. Freedom of speech is a right guaranteed by the U.S. Constitution. As with all other constitutional rights, then, freedom of speech is an American privilege and responsibility. So citizen, identify yourself and then speak so that other citizens may hear your claims, make judgments about your reasoning and the validity of what you say. In doing so, your fellow citizens may choose to use their freedom of speech to challenge your ideas.

Lately, in America and on our campus, too many have been saying that since Americans have freedom of expression, there is nothing to be done. That's why we sometimes end up with the odd situation that when someone makes ugly racial, anti-gay and lesbian, anti-some-group statements, people act as if there is nothing to be done. Lately, we have been acting as if we think that the right to free-expression means that we have to shut up in the face of someone else's ugly, hateful words. No we don't...

No we don't because no one has a right to free expression. In America, we have a right to freedom of speech. All of us have that right.

Starting at 8 p.m. Tuesday, August 16, 2011, on the campus of NCSU we had an event called "Respect the Pack." That event was put on to protest and challenge all the offensive, negative group-hate graffiti that shows up in the Free Expression Tunnel. Our protest that night was significant. We were expressing our freedom of speech to say that we value each and every student on our campus. We were expressing our freedom of speech to say that when someone writes racial graffiti, that does not reflect the opinion of the whole campus. When students at NCSU recognize and understand that one student's freedom of speech does not negate other students' freedom of speech, students will realize that means there is something to be done.

We can raise our voices in opposition to group-hate.

****

There is something else here to be curious about. People keep saying to me that this generation of young people, your generation, is used to diversity. *"They have never seen segregation. They have always interacted with people who are not like them. It's not a problem for them."* If that is true, then I have to ask: In young people, where does the group-hate on our campus, the group-hate we should protest, come from?

Here's something else some of the Wolfpack do not understand. Whatever your skins color, your ethnic background, your religion, without being aware of it, as an American you have received training in racial matters. In ways that you are not aware of you have been socialized to think about race in a particular way. When I say this in class, some students are jolted by memories.

One said that when their grandfather gave them a nut they asked what kind of nut is this. He said, "It's a Brazil nut, but we call them *nigger-toes.*" An African American female student said that she and her friends used to say let's go *nigger-knocking*, completely unaware of the hate-filled, violent origin of that phrase. You see, many of you have been led to believe the lie that race never was a "...big deal."

To give my students a realistic picture of the history of the big deal of race in America, I show them the blood. I have my students read a witnessed history of the 1960s Civil Rights Movement: Tim Tyson's "Blood Done Sign My Name." Tyson tells the story of a racial murder in Oxford, NC. From the dust jacket the potential reader learns:

> *On May 11, 1970, Henry Marrow, a 23-year-old black veteran, walked into a crossroads store owned by Robert Teel, a rough man with a criminal record and ties to the Ku Klux Klan and came out running. Teel and two of his sons chased Marrow, beat him unmercifully, and killed him in public as he pleaded for his life. In the words of a prosecutor: "They shot him like you or I would kill a snake."*
>
> *Like many small Southern Towns, Oxford [NC] had barely been touched by the civil rights movement. But in the wake of the killing, young African Americans took to the streets, led by 22-year-old Ben Chavis, a future president of the NAACP. As mass protests crowded the town square, a cluster of returning Vietnam veterans organized what one termed "a military operation." While lawyers battled in the courthouse that summer in a drama that one termed "a Perry Mason kind of thing," the Ku Klux Klan raged in*

the shadows and black veterans torched the town's tobacco warehouses."

Tyson describes the racial context up from slavery to the modern civil rights movement, but not in a standard way. As the son of Vernon Tyson, pastor of Oxford, NC's all-white Methodist church, 10-year-old white boy Tim Tyson experienced the tensions in Oxford that resulted from the racial murder of Henry Marrow in 1970. So Tyson's witnessed history is the anchor for the general history.

I never lecture on the book. Instead, I have the students read the book "on the side," a third of Tyson's book at a time (1st third: pp. 1-177. 2nd third: 118-246. 3rd third: 247-325). After reading each third, students turn in to me a typed personal reaction.

Tyson's book surprises my students:

> *"I was surprised that the racial climate was like this in 1970. Such racial prejudice is a characteristic of the decades before the death of Marrow but one does not associate such attitudes and actions with the time of the occurrence. When learning about the racial past of the U.S. as a child I was learning what can only be called the cliff notes of past race relations. I was taught only about the events of the 'Civil Rights Movement' and nothing about the everyday race relations before, during, and after the 'Civil Rights' years. My reaction to most of the information that is presented in this book is surprise. I was not aware of the historical facts that Tyson present and the presence of this information now allows me to have a more critical look at the country's racial history and race relations of today."*

My students, female, white, black, brown, Iranian, East-Indian, Chinese-American, Lebanese, male, have these kinds of reactions to Tyson's book. For my students here at North Carolina State University, part of the impact of the book has to do with the fact that the racial murder of Henry Marrow happened in Oxford, NC. On that point, one student wrote:

"The story told in <u>Blood</u> is… a story I've heard so many times before and this time it's seemingly all new. The story is one told to me by my family and other individuals that lived it. The perspective from which it is told gives me some insight into how this situation played out in the eyes of someone looking from the other side. This is honestly the first time I've ever seen a racially motivated killing and Jim Crow South in general told from the perspective of someone who is white. I've had white teachers and friends in the past tell me a little bit about the rioting and the desegregation of public places but nothing that truly gave me a glimpse from their perspective. This story hits home more so than most of the others I've heard because this isn't a story about life in the 'Deep South'; this is a story about North Carolina. Places mentioned in the story like Statesville, Monroe, Salisbury and Wilmington are places I frequent. Charlotte is my home; I've been to the Temple Beth-El and I had no idea that it was almost destroyed. These are the kinds of stories people need to know before they say North Carolina isn't that bad or racism is gone in NC."

That local connection is important. My students begin to see that racial unrest did not just happen "…over there."

Racial unrest happened right here in North Carolina.

****

Outraged, stunned, in total disbelief about how much they don't know, my students are captivated by this history. Then my students experience a psychological tension.

> *"As I read the middle portion of the book I came to the realization that part of what makes it such an effective narrative is the perspective from which it is written. While I find the middle part of the book more 'history heavy' than the first, Tyson continues the practice of including events and descriptions to which it is easy to personally relate. These inclusions seem to anchor the narrative and make it easier for me to view it as [the real experiences of] a specific person, rather than a simple narration of past events. The rich descriptions of the persons involved also make the history seem more 'real,' with those involved seeming less like actors and more like people with their own hopes, wishes, motivations, and failings. This emphasizes the idea that many of the people described in <u>Blood</u> are products of the time and society in which they lived rather than reducing them to pure labels such as 'murderous white racist' or 'black terrorist.' This is part of what makes <u>Blood</u> so powerful; Tyson forces the reader to a level that requires him to see the events as more than just marks on a timeline."*

That complication creates a new personal connection that has the important effect of causing students to ask, "…what would I have done?" Any number of students asked that question directly. One wrote:

> *"…In chapter nine, I must say that I learned a lot about the individuals who played a part in the 'military*

operations' at Oxford. This chapter seemed to highlight the struggle of the revolution itself, the mixed ideas and ideals of the different peoples and what eventually occurred.

While reading I felt myself wanting to encourage the uprising movement. I asked myself what I would have done if I were there right now. Would I march, protest, eat dinner, make friends, and fight for and with the African Americans or would I fear for my life and be swept away by the white supremacy?

These are tough questions for me, and I know what I want to answer in today's terms, but would I really do that if I were in their world. Yes, I do believe it was a different world then and truthfully I cannot say for sure what I would do. And that fact alone evokes confusion and a feeling I don't know how to put into words."

Painful as are these self-examinations, NCSU students in my class want this experience. I say this because often, in our classroom discussions, students bring up their reading of "Blood" to express anger and disappointment that they were not exposed to the real story of race in America and the modern civil rights movement until they got to college. Anger and disappointment that one student put this way:

"Moving away from Tyson's school experiences, the next thing to put a rocket under my butt was the Wilmington Race Riot. Pardon my language, but holy crap! I have grown up in North Carolina, and have always taken an interest in school, and everything the teachers taught. In elementary school, I was on the African American Quiz Bowl Team for four years... and in that time combined with all the outside-of-school readings I have done, and the in-school

42

schooling I have received, I had never heard of these Wilmington Race Riot. I am by no means an ignorant person, and quite honestly, the fact that I have never heard of [that riot] worries me.

What if not very many people have heard of this riot? The school system is doing a great disservice to us, the students, at that point by not giving us the full story. Are they trying to erase the record? Because blood stains, no matter how much you try to wash it out... The only way to avoid repeating the past is to learn from our history."

Maybe students are not exposed to the truth in middle and high school because adults want to protect their childhood. Or maybe teachers do not expose students to the harsh, yet relatively recent, American racial history, because students will ask the teacher, where were you? What did you do?

But avoiding tough questions, smoothing over what really happened, prevents real learning. Learning, it turns out, takes tension and conflict. On matters of race in America, despite the growls it causes, students want to know how it was really.

As my students read "Blood," they have a powerful psychological experience; one so powerful it leads to... well, it leads to this:

"The reporter penned that a 'sham and mockery of justice' had been committed (p. 245). He could not have stated the truth more blatantly. As I read the verdict from the all-white jury my eyes welled up with tears. I threw the book in defiance of such a terrible event. All I could think about was that the entire trial was complete bullshit."

At this point these NCSU students are in the midst of a transformation of their motivation. Now when those students think about race, they are motivated to see the issues from both sides. How do my interests coordinate with the interests of the person who is not a member of my racial group? It is almost impossible for these students to ask, "...why are *they* making this such a big deal?"

By the time they reach the end of the book, all of my students have become open to more information, and motivated to seek that information. One wrote:

> *"The details Tyson goes into while describing the events and histories of people involved help paint a very vivid picture of the times in which he grew up and the people who played an important role in his life and the lives of everyone who stood for equal rights. I already have a very distinct vision in my head of the scenes that unfolded on that fateful night. No historical piece of literature has grabbed my attention and interested me as much as this book. I'm not one who typically enjoys any kind of history lesson at all, which is why it's so amazing to me that the 246 pages that we've read so far have inspired me to visit the setting in which the book takes place."*

Sometimes a student experienced a stunned mix of emotion that pushed them into quiet but deep reflection.

> *"When I first started <u>Blood</u> I would best describe myself as confused, horrified, and troubled. As I've continued reading, those feelings have in no way dissipated, but have evolved into amazement, empathy, intrigue, and respect. I put down the book one evening and caught myself staring at the cover blankly. I wasn't looking at the picture. I was sorting through my thoughts. Oh man did I have some thoughts and questions."*

A new insight was close:

> *"My overall view of the civil rights movement is changing through the course of the book, as I learn the historical truth that has been covered up with politically correct wishes. We are led to believe that a few devout white supremacists begrudgingly accepted equal rights after all the moderates went right along with the movement. Not only is it not true, but also it ignores the fascinating struggle that really went much deeper than a few public demonstrations. Equality was fought for by burning the tobacco warehouses and other economic and civil disruption. It was not all a peaceful plea for equal rights, it was a true struggle. This is something that is often forgotten when looking at the evolution of civil rights in America."*

Reading a true story of race in America led to new appreciation. My students find themselves engaged in a full reevaluation of, and growing respect for, the hard work and different tactics it had taken to begin the difficult change of the racial environment of America. By reading "Blood" my students had been brought from racial ignorance and naïveté to a balanced view of reality.

Tyson's book, "Blood Done Sign My Name" helps create a new knowledge base for my students about why race can be such a tension-based big deal in interpersonal interaction. Together the class and the book jolt them. One student put her feelings this way:

> *"This book made me feel bipolar. I would get really angry, and would feel really sad/bad because I would begin to understand the character. Mixed feelings between hatred and pity came back and forth often. Adding on to my bipolar-like commotion, I often*

pondered and meditated upon my own actions; kind of like a monk. Now, I have three reasons to dislike this book. Firstly, it illustrates the tragic reality of 1970s too well, and secondly, it made me feel kind of bipolar. Lastly, it makes me think and reflect upon myself repeatedly; I think this monk-like behavior will become a part of me for a long time."

But what is the content of that monk-like behavior? What are these members of the Wolfpack reflecting on and to what end? One student answered that in terms of the most powerful moment, the most powerful insight she had when reading "Blood." She wrote:

...the true moment, the one that hit me like a ton of bricks, came towards the end of the epilogue. When Tyson wrote, "That history reveals that blood that has signed every one of our names. The sacrifice has already been made, in the bottoms of slave ships, in the portals of Ellis Island, in the tobacco fields of North Carolina and the sweatshops of New York City." I could not help it, I broke down crying. I realized not only was I ignorant of the past of others, but also my own past.

My mother's side of the family is predominantly from Ireland. They came over on ships hoping for a better life, passed through those portals at Ellis Island, and instead were probably treated like crap. I have no real idea of what they endured or what their life was like. And I know that in many ways it cannot even begin to compare to the terrors that those who were brought over in the bottom of slave ships, and whose families for generations afterward, even when freed from the bonds of slavery, were not treated as equals.

This was the part where it really became clear to me, that everyone today is living with their own history. We all have our own cultural frame of reference, as we've learned, and though I can probably never truly understand what it means to be in that frame of reference, I can at least attempt to put myself inside it, acknowledge that it exists.

Black children growing up today, while not experiencing first-hand the racism we just read about, are growing up with parents who did. In so many ways people don't have history, <u>they are history</u>. Walking, talking histories interacting with one another...

That was what I really took from this book. The past is here, it looms over us whether or not we know or understand it. The past drives the actions of the present and determines the outcomes of the future. To ignore our past is a grave mistake because it ensures that we cannot learn from it or build from it. We don't need to obsess over it, or demand apologies from people who had nothing to do with the injustice, or feel guilty about deeds we did not commit, but we cannot distance ourselves from it. We cannot forget.

To do that would be a huge disservice to all those who fought to right the wrongs of their pasts, to make a better foundation for future generations to build on. If we do not acknowledge their sacrifices, how can we understand how precious the opportunities we have today are, and at what cost we have them. No, we must never forget.

Once my students get that, they stop growling.
They have been fed.
They have learned the truth.
They have knowledge of the big deal.
Fed, but now with a new hunger, they howl.

Listen… listen.

Chapter Four:

Catching Fire

"We live by story."

So says the writer Richard Rhodes.[3] Later in his book about the writing life, Mr. Rhodes says:

> "Story enlightens us... Story is the primary vehicle human beings use to structure knowledge and experience."[4]

In my "Interpersonal Relationships and Race" course, I teach students the major theory of how relationships develop[5], and then a lot of social psychological concepts about social interaction and intergroup anxiety. But to bring the social psychological concepts to life I tell stories. I use stories to illustrate and elaborate the concept, the theory, to make my point. Sometimes I have planned to use a particular story, sometimes a story occurs to me in the midst of a class discussion.

On the second day of class, Spring 2012, I was getting my students to tell me what topics and questions they hoped we

---

[3] Rhodes, R. (1995) (p. 1). How to write: Advice and reflections. New York: Harper Collins.

[4] Ibid; p. 197.

[5] Kelley, H.H. & Thibaut, J.W. (1978). Interpersonal Relationships: A theory of interdependence. New York: John Wiley.

would get to discuss in the class. Someone asked about so-called subtle racism. And right then I thought of a story.

What popped into my head was something that happened in my introduction to social psychology class (Psych 311). So I told the story:

> *In Psych 311, as some of you know, students have to write a one-page paper. The assignment is to write about "...what one new thought you have had about interpersonal relationships as a result of what you learned in this course." As you can imagine, I get a lot of different, interesting, papers. One concept that a lot of people write about is "autistic friendliness," which is a rigid predisposition to be friendly. It's what people do to get along especially early in a relationship. Saying they like a type of movie, music, food that they really don't care for or know anything about. People do this to avoid conflict; they do everything they can to appear easy to get along with. A rigid predisposition to be friendly.*
>
> *A lot of students in Psych 311 write about how learning about this has helped them do better at the beginning of a relationship by avoiding that tendency to be rigidly friendly. Well, in the Spring of 2010 I noticed something. Many of those writing about this tendency said something like, "I never realized that telling little white lies could cause so much trouble. But now that I know, I will avoid telling those little white lies."*
>
> *There were way too many papers that referred to "...little white lies." So I called the class out on this. In the final lecture, I said to my class, "...way too many of you talked about autistic friendliness as telling '...little white lies.' Lies that you thought were harmless, you called white. And you were so comfortable saying this, it never occurred to you to think about the fact that the*

person who would be reading your paper would be a big, giant, dark-skinned, black man. Isn't that interesting... white lies... really... so the really bad lies are...

Turns out they are all lies. That's the shining black truth.

I told that story off the cuff, simply because it popped into my head when a certain question was asked. After telling the "white lies" story, I said to students in my race class, *"But the question is how did it come to pass that so-called small lies are referred to as 'white?'"* Then I asked, *"Is that what some people think of as subtle racism? Well we'll see..."*

I told the story, used the story to raise a question, and we moved on.

As a professor, I never know for sure everything that will have impact. At the end of the Spring 2012 semester, when my students turned in their final paper, I began to hear the growls of the Wolfpack turn into howls. One student wrote:

Sitting here, trying to determine what I consider to be the most important new thought about interpersonal-intergroup interactions and relationships is proving very difficult. I have felt that with each session I have become more of a complete person. I became very aware of my prejudices and own stereotyping. I have thoroughly enjoyed this academic journey but I feel the value in this course is not papers or tests but the quiet revolution we are wishing to start. One thing that has stuck out to me is the term "neo diversity." In short, neo diversity is the multidimensional social change in our society. We live in this age of neo-diversity and it affects everyone. Things started to occur to me throughout this course that I had never really thought about. For example, the idea behind white lie. How is it that no one has ever

51

told us what that stands for yet we all know what a white lie is? Things like this started to unravel before me, leaving me confused and curious.

You can hear this young white man saying, "…what the…?" At the end of the semester, students who have been in my "Interpersonal Relationships and Race" course have a heightened sensitivity and a new understanding of what is going on. Neo-diversity. They get it. One student wrote:

Living in America there is no way around interacting with others who do not look like you. Our world is primarily social; America in itself is one of diversity, which can create a lot of anxiety amongst many of us. Neo-Diversity. What does this mean? Neo Diversity is the new social uncertainty brought about by the ongoing, rapid, and substantive social changes, and can commonly be defined by a phrase "Who are among the 'we' and who are among the 'they.'" Our world is not a stagnant world but one that is continuously changing. And more specifically, Neo Diversity effect can be defined as an interracial encounter that has many possible outcomes and are not well defined which can create unpredictability.

This effect can be seen day to day in our society, and I felt like this was the one new thought that was the most important. In any given situation one will encounter someone of another race throughout the day, whether it is grocery shopping, pumping gas, going to class, a student gathering… you get the point.

A place that I find the most interracial interaction is when someone is at work; I have experienced this first hand. I am a manager at a clothing store, and had stationed one of my sales associates at the front door to greet our customers as they entered. I noticed a woman who came in who was wearing her native clothing, commonly called a Hajab or Burka. When the woman entered the store, the "greeter" did not greet her as they have done to others that have entered. I simply went to my sales associate and asked why she had not greeted the woman. Her response was simply, "I didn't know what I was supposed to say." After a small conversation, she admitted that she had never, in person, seen someone of that race and it shocked her.

After taking this course it is now evident that the sales associate was experiencing the Neo Diversity Effect and was uncertain of the possible outcomes of offering the greeting.

But we have to ask, what shocked the greeter? Was it what the female customer was wearing? The Hajib? Or was it what the greeter took the Hajib to mean? What assumptions were at work here, and were so powerful that it stopped the greeter from simply greeting, simply speaking to another person?

Many of you know the old saying about assumptions. When you assume, you make an ass out of you and me. It's always true and it is a critical truth to the survival of any interaction, any relationship, especially in these neo-diverse times. Turns out one of the concepts my students learn has to do with assumptions we make about what other people believe. One young white man wrote:

This class has, over the duration of the semester, shaped and molded how I perceive interpersonal-intergroup dynamics and relationships, and subsequently has impressed a marked influence on my behavior and approach to such interactions. The teaching of theoretical concepts has naturally overflowed into practical application in my life; the course has apprenticed me through the nurturing domain of theory and conceptualization, and, as a knight with a new weapon, has sent me out into the battlefield to slice through the prejudice, stereotyping, and misperceptions that pervade my daily life. This class is not merely a course on interpersonal-intergroup theory, but a course on life.

As I reflect on the many ways that this class and its theoretical concepts have affected me, there is one concept that lay at the forefront of my recollection: Rokeach's Belief-Congruence Hypothesis. Out of all the theoretical concepts discussed, this one particularly resonated with me. Knowledge of this concept illuminated the dark haze that lingered between me and interracial interactions; it opened my eyes to my own prejudices, my own faults.

You see, although I have experienced much exposure throughout my life to interracial interactions, I still found them somewhat troublesome... because of anxiety or apprehensiveness. As the Belief-Congruence theory hypothesizes, it is not the matter of race directly that arouses this anxiety within me, but instead the exaggerated assumption of belief differences between the members of other races and myself. In reality, however, these assumptions serve as an invisible barrier; it is fallacious to treat an individual as a group, and dangerous to transfer erroneous attributions from the group to its individual members. Further, the assumed incongruence of beliefs on which I stood in security was entirely imaginative.

So, given this newfound knowledge, I have entirely shifted my attitude when approaching interracial interactions: I commit to wiping the slate clean and interacting with the individual based on the individual, rather than their racial group. I no longer feel the persistent apprehension that pervaded the interracial interactions of my past. I have eliminated the supremacy of misguided assumptions, and have taken reign over my thoughts and behaviors in interpersonal-intergroup interactions.

And I am so much better off.

Others also took the lesson of the belief congruence hypothesis to heart. A Punjabi Indian American student wrote:

It's not always easy to interact with those that are different from yourself and especially when they are of a different race. There are so many things that could go wrong in the interaction and I always worry that I could say something that might offend that person I am interacting with. I often used to and still sometimes find myself relying on stereotypes about people's race and how I could use this information to interact with them. I try to find some kind of similarity in that person so I can relate to them but what I never realized was that by trying to use that shortcut, I was making assumptions and this could lead to a bigger problem.

In class this year I have learned about the Belief Congruence Hypothesis which states: in so far as psychological process are involved <u>assumptions</u> of belief similarity or dissimilarity are more important as causes of social discrimination than racial or ethnic group membership per se. After learning about this concept it got me thinking about the things I think about and say when talking to people of a different race or ethnicity. It made me realize that the assumptions I make about a person based on race are often not correct.

Being in this class also made me realize how I think about people. I remember when I met one of my close friends, just because she looked like she was

Indian I was inclined to talk to her. Later when I learned she was not in fact Indian, I tried to find other similar situations or topics to talk to her about so that we could develop a good relationship. In this situation there were some things I said out of assumptions and this made my friend step back a little and reevaluate our friendship. I tried to use the similarities we had and made assumptions about her religion and background. However, when I learned my assumptions actually were incorrect and offended her I realized I had a problem and at that time I didn't know exactly how to handle the situation.

Now that I understand what exactly took place in that interaction, I know not to make such mistakes again. Assumptions make us think we know what we are talking about but in reality these assumptions can cause great psychological tension between the two people. Using this information I learned in class I will be able to handle interactions between myself and those of different races better.

I know because I am a minority (Punjabi-Indian-American) I will have to know how to interact with those different from myself everyday and learning how to go about having positive interactions is very important. By using the Belief Congruence Hypothesis I can avoid making assumptions of similarity or differences between people because now I have learned that making these assumptions are more important causes of discrimination than even race and ethnicity. I will be careful to not assume things and I am more open to learning about different people and their backgrounds before I put my stereotypes and assumptions in play within an interaction.

To some, learning about the role of the belief congruence effect was like biting into spoiled food. A female student put it this way:

The Belief Congruence Hypothesis that we learned in class was the most influential theoretical concept for me. In other words, the social distance that members of in-groups create between themselves and members of out-groups is a psychological process of making assumptions about the out-group member's beliefs, and furthermore making the assumption that those beliefs are different from the in-group member's beliefs. Basically, the issue is not that you don't look like me, but rather, when I look at you, I assume that your beliefs are different than mine.

I had never thought about race relations in this way before. Yes, I understood the irrationality of discriminating against someone on the basis of their skin color, but I couldn't come up with an explanation for the continuation of this ludicrousness, other than just plain ignorance. However, this hypothesis suggests that it is much deeper. It is not that we have dumbly developed an aversion to a particular skin pigment, but rather, we have learned to use skin color as an indicator of the character and morality of a person. When I stepped back and broke it down like this to myself, I felt disgusted.

We discussed the absurdity of the claim, "I see don't see skin color." Isn't the claim, "I can see your beliefs just by observing your skin color," just as illogical? It is essentially robbing out-group members of the chance to show their true identity. I can truly say that after learning about this concept, I will continue to consider the beliefs of individuals in all of my interpersonal relationships, both intergroup and intragroup, above their racial and ethnic look. I will also make a strong effort to share this meaningful ideal with others.

Writing as if she has heard all that has come before, and that she is writing the concluding summary, one student wrote:

Why should I let one social difference fill me with so much anxiety that I end up having false interactions with others? No matter whom I am interacting with autistic-friendliness is never the way to go, that point was made quite clear in Social Psychology class. If I am honest with myself and present myself truthfully the other person I am interacting with then they too can feel comfortable to be who they are while interacting. Just being accepting of who I am and accepting the fact that the person I am interacting with is going to be different from me no matter what their race, is a major step to overcoming that anxiety.

Race may be a more prevalent difference that can be noticed right away in some cases, but even if someone is the same race as me they are still a completely different person with completely different opinions, so the possibility of having a negative interaction in that case is still present. The color of someone's skin does not determine whether we share the similar values, beliefs, likes, or dislikes.

Plus, worrying about saying something offensive is only going to make offensive thoughts come to mind. If I just go into interactions from now on with a positive attitude and presenting myself as I truly am I know I am much more likely to have positive interactions with anyone I decide to be social with.

Once you learn something, once it hits you personally, you have a responsibility to act on it. That at least is what my

students say to me in their papers. Now that I know, they say...
"Now that I know." A male student wrote:

Turns out we aren't as concerned with how much people look like ourselves as much as we are concerned with whether or not they think like ourselves. We do not treat others differently because they are different than what we are used to, we treat them differently because we assume they are not thinking the same way we are, <u>because</u> they are different than we are.

When meeting someone of a different race or ethnicity, we make the assumption that because they are different on the outside, they must operate differently on the inside as well. The idea that they are not thinking the same way we are is what causes the tension; we assume they are thinking differently than us, which creates an unknown that we do not know how to react to. Therefore, we revert back to stereotypes of the group, stereotypes that are an attempt to guess what they must be thinking, because surely it is different than what we are.

I obviously had felt the feeling of tension associated with interacting with an out-group before. We all have. However, I had never thought about that tension being associated with the idea that the other person did not operate under the same beliefs and/or goals as me. It seems to me that some of the tension that these interactions create could be alleviated by making note of some larger goals that we may share.

We might be in line at the bar, trying to get a drink.

We might be in class, trying to do well on a group project.

Or we could just be bored and uncomfortable, looking for someone to talk to.

It seems that if you can focus on some belief that is shared among the two people of different ethnicity then the two people will be able to operate with less tension than if it was just focusing on outward appearance.

****

People live life at the interpersonal level. Watch a person walk into a room and see a friend and you see that person's eyes light up and a smile spread across their face. It is as if seeing someone you know flips a switch and now life moves through you. But watch a person walk into a room and there are only strangers there. What do people do? Eyes scan the room quickly then are aimed down at the floor, and the person moves to find an empty seat or they just walk out of the room. A different switch is flipped. This one turns off life, seems to almost kill the interpersonal moment. About that, one female student wrote:

Once I learned about the belief congruence effect, I began noticing when I was walking around and saw someone I did not know and looked different than me I immediately, without realizing it, strictly saw the difference between me and the other person. It is not so much to do with the race or ethnic group that I assume they identify with but I would almost make up little stories about people based on me not knowing them and judging their overall demeanor. It is not that the person does not look like me but that it is when I look at the other person I assume that he/she does not act or believe like I do. This sets up a terrible start to a potential relationship when this happens. A relationship is formed when people's belief systems are coordinated. Yet with assumptions of belief dissimilarity there is no chance to belief coordination.

It is a strange and anxious feeling to catch yourself in once you know exactly what is going on and why it is going on. And on the same hand it is quite difficult to not fall into this realm and it takes a lot of long, hard and deliberate focus to be aware of the forces that are acting upon me and my mind during this age of social uncertainty.

All of this nervousness and anxiety that surrounds each and every person is due to the neo-diversity age that we live in. There are no set rules and regulations on how to interact with people that are different from us. I will try and better myself through all the information this course has provided us but for me the belief-congruence effect has to be one of the most important concepts to be aware of because it has a domino effect in successfully being mentally aware of what is attacking our minds. When there is a believed (assumed) belief-difference... many people back away and keep a social distance which helps explain why people are still segregating themselves even without segregation laws.

Stereotypes will always be around and relied on by many unaware and even aware people but it is up to those who are enlightened to its power over people to consciously fight it within and teach the equality of all people. The belief-congruence hypothesis has made it very apparent to me that it is useless to rely on stereotypes dealing with belief systems. It sets up a whole new ballgame when I start to see the similarities between myself and a person that I see or when I meet a stranger. I am very appreciative of learning this.

This student's profound point about segregation is worth repeating. She wrote: *When there is a believed (assumed) belief-difference... many people back away and keep a social distance which helps explain why people are still segregating themselves even without segregation laws.*

Yet in the age of neo-diversity, keeping social distance by limiting your interactions to one group takes real work. One black male student wrote:

> *One interaction that is fairly notable to me occurred while on the job, at Han-Dee Hugo's. This is a convenience store so I interact with a vast number of different people throughout the day. One particular day toward the end of the midday rush last month, a white male came through the door. I noticed him because I expected him to walk toward my register considering the fact that he would be the next one to be helped. So I nodded at him and asked if I could help him and with not even a hint of acknowledgment from him, he walked all the way across my register to the only other register in the store, which happened to have a family in line shopping as if they were taking a long trip.*
>
> *I began to think that the guy either was in no type of rush at all to get his gas or he did not like black people. He had on billed cap with a t-shirt and dingy jeans, looked over the age of 40; along with the enormous Ford 1-150 I saw him pull up in, so immediately I turned to the conclusion that this guy did not like black people. My coworker pointed the man in my direction telling him that I was open and as soon as he heard those words he looked up at me and gave a look of reluctance that basically said, "I can't believe I have to go to this line."*
>
> *He never looked at me the entire time that he was telling me how much gas he wanted or the Wintergreen Grizzly long-cut chewing tobacco. His head was down, not counting money I should add, and his arms were crossed as well. I rang up the gas and asked if he*

needed anything else and still no response. He never answered any question I directed to him from the time he walked in until he left. The total of his purchases ended up being just at $24. Now I saw him reach for his wallet to count money and while I had my hand stuck out for the cash he placed every bill on the counter in front of me.

I was genuinely insulted.

He acted like I was not there the whole time I tried to help him with his transaction so me being as stubborn and competitive as I am, stood there with my hand out as if I did not see the money on the counter. After a couple of seconds he pointed to the money and said "There you go, I want my stuff." In this case I had no choice since there were people behind him that I had to checkout so I picked up the money from the counter and counted out his change. I took the bills and change that I owed him, along with the tobacco, and placed it on the counter in front of him. He mistakenly had his hand out and I stepped back and told him, "Have a nice day...may I help the next person."

He walked out.

To repeat myself, in this age of neo-diversity, keeping social distance by limiting your interactions to one group takes real work. You can't even buy gas without there being some chance of you having to have an intergroup moment of interaction. That is the general state of neo-diversity America. No way to even attempt intergroup avoidance on a university campus. On our NCSU campus, there are all kinds of people by religion, ethnicity, sexual orientation, gender and race. Walking across campus, sitting in a classroom of 200, eating in a cafeteria, standing in line for coffee at Port City Java, no one can avoid seeing students who do not look like them. It's not possible. So that means the work of staying segregated becomes psychological.

You have to work to prevent normal social interaction from occurring; to stop yourself from saying hi to the person standing behind or in front of you in line for coffee or sitting in class next to you. How do students do this? Not only by assuming belief differences, but by using a way of talking about people that further creates distance. A female student wrote:

> *Before this class, if I would hear people using racial slurs or treat members of a different race differently than their own, I would freely call those people racist and say they were prejudice. I would not say these things to their faces but I still held the thoughts. These types of slips made me feel happy with myself because I was not one of those people who used racial slurs, but the longer I am in this class, the more I see how I too have used racial slurs and know more racial slurs than I ever realized. I am half Mexican but I look white and because of this, sometimes I would use racial slurs against Mexicans. I am Mexican so it is not as offensive, right?*
>
> *Of course, now I have learned that just because people use racial slurs does not mean they are in fact a racist or a bigot. We have been introduced to so much history, hatred, racial slurs, our family's thoughts on race, etc., without even realizing. Because of this, when we interact with different people that we are unfamiliar with we become anxious, and everything we [have been told; we have heard] about that particular race is brought to the forefront and interactions can go terribly wrong.*

Yes, at the speed of light, life at the interpersonal level can go terribly wrong. Interactions can get out of hand so fast.

We consider this in my class. We identify what it takes for an interaction to go from a casual "...hey, how's it going" to a heated "...what did you say to me?" One young man wrote about he learned about this dynamic. He wrote:

> *If I must pick one idea that has taught me the most, I would have to choose the levels-of-interdependence hypothesis. The hypothesis states that, "Whenever social interaction creates or intensifies interpersonal anxiety, the interaction dynamic of the dyad will quickly shift from a focus on behaviors to a focus on the beliefs and identities of the two people in the interaction."*
>
> *In more plain English, this hypothesis states that interpersonal anxiety can set an interaction on fire. This happens when one party, or both parties, feel anxiety and try to be overly chummy in order to extinguish their inner tension. Since neither party actually knows the other party very well, they are left to grope around amongst their stereotypes to try to find something to talk about. In the case of an in-group and an out-group interaction, this often results with one party resorting to using a stereotype to facilitate a conversation. My new thought from this class is that many people who use stereotypes are not prejudiced, but are experiencing anxiety and are left confused with how to deal with their inner tension.*
>
> *When interpersonal anxiety comes into the interaction, the anxiety is palpable to both parties. This anxiety leads to the use of stereotypes more than actual prejudice does. In my personal interactions I deal with stereotypes quite a bit. As a Pakistani-American, I get the full range of Arab and Middle-Eastern stereotypes. Normally when I hear these stereotypes thrown at me, I tend to get very upset. This is normal because an*

intergroup interaction can be very emotional for both parties in the dyad. An ill-spoken comment can kill a relationship before it starts, and this has happened with me personally on numerous occasions. However, I never once thought about the intergroup anxiety that can be triggered by meeting someone of a different race or ethnicity. Even though we live in an age of neo-diversity, we still don't have enough explicit rules for intergroup interactions. This uncertainty leads to anxiety, which can lead to poor decisions and inappropriate comments.

This class has taught me to be more patient in the face of intergroup anxiety. I now understand that the use of stereotypes may not represent a certain prejudice in a person, but rather may reflect their anxiety and nervousness. I will try to remain calm when I hear stereotypes and will try to work with the other person in my dyad to work through our intergroup anxiety. Of course, this will only work if the other person allows it to. However, no longer will I be the person who allows an interaction to fail due to intergroup anxiety.

So when anxiety enters an interaction, the interaction can catch fire. By the way, that doesn't mean that this only happens in an interaction between people from different groups. One of the interaction-burning features of neo-diversity is not being able to know who believes what, even among members of our own racial group. That's one of the things we all struggle with because of neo-diversity. We can't easily answer the question, "Who are the 'we' and who are among the 'they?'" We sit down with people who all look like us and we assume belief similarity. And because of that assumption, the interaction speeds up so fast and gets so hot it bursts into flames. One Caucasian American young man wrote:

Here's what happened: it was an ordinary weekend night during this semester and I had gone over to a friend's apartment to have a few drinks and hang out. There were four other guys there, two of them were some of my best friends from middle and high school (we'll say Mike and Zach) and another guy was the younger brother of one of those best friends (Todd). Todd was the only person who did not drink that night as he never has. I was fairly good friends with the Todd as well. The night was going along in an ordinary fashion and everyone who was drinking was probably a few beers in. The conversation turned to reminiscing about times in middle school. We mentioned one kid named Andy specifically and how he was notorious for making racist jokes and how that was our first encounter with him. Andy ended up being a friend of ours through high school and Zach actually told us the first joke he remembered hearing from Andy. He got done and I felt uncomfortable, everyone else laughed and I cracked a halfhearted smile and said, "...man, so racist." It was not a defensive or angry tone that I used and Zach quickly replied, "Yeah but that's pretty funny" at this point there really was no tension and everyone still had a smile on their face. I replied back, "yeah but Andy's pretty racist."

I now interrupt this story for *"BREAKING NEWS."*

One of the things I teach in my class is that there are differences between prejudice, bigotry and racism. I have to teach the differences because the word "...racism" is thrown around with so much inaccuracy that it has lost its real meaning.

Racism is institutional; racism is never in a person. Prejudice resides in individuals as "...just because" negative feelings toward some group, males, females, African Americans, Hispanics, you know the idea. Must prejudice be visible to

67

others? No. A well-socialized person can have prejudices that never show up in their behavior.

Bigotry is what we have when a prejudice comes out in behavior. Outward use of gender slurs, racial slurs, and ethnic slurs is bigotry. Making a decision to discriminate based on one's prejudice is bigotry. Avoiding interaction with a person of a certain group, because of your negative feelings about the group, is bigotry.

When we see those old pictures of whites yelling at, spitting at, beating African Americans, we are seeing bigotry. Outward hostility and violence from white individuals toward black individuals was the face of racism, but not racism itself. Racism was the laws and customs of the society that supported and encouraged bigotry. Racism was what gave white individuals the level of comfort and safety white's felt showing their bigotry. Racism occurs by way of institutional, societal, authorization.

Racism is always institutional, organizational and societal[6]. When laws of a society or customs of an organization actively, or through indifference, support and encourage individual bigotry, we have racism. And since those institutional, organization, societal policies and laws have been outlawed, we have to deal with the remnants, the leftovers of racism. Racial slurs are that. Racial slurs are part of the leftovers, the legacy of racism.

As always, I will keep you informed of any other *BREAKING NEWS*. But now, back to our story, still in progress where our story teller is saying:

"...yeah but Andy's pretty racist."
I was being extremely cautious not to offend anyone or use a condescending tone. Zach again replied

---

[6] Simpson, G.E. & Yinger, J.M. (1985). Racial and Cultural Minorities: An analysis of prejudice and discrimination. New York: Plenum Publishers.

something along the lines of, "I mean it's a joke and it's funny. Plus it's not like we mean it." I explained to him, "Even if you think it's funny and you're not being intentionally degrading, it's still bigoted behavior to engage in." The conversation was friendly and nobody was going at each other's throats or anything. There was probably twenty minutes of back in forth. All three of my good friends were all backing each other and the fourth guy was sitting awkwardly not saying anything at all (everyone present was Caucasian by the way). I was claiming that I didn't think they were racist and I didn't care if they made the jokes, just that the actual telling of the jokes was a form of racist/bigoted behavior. They contended that it was not. Some of the excuses I heard went along the lines of:

"I have black friends, I'm not racist." and "I say 'Nigga' to some of my black friends all the time."

"I think it's funny and I'm not being serious."

"Other people don't get to determine if I'm being serious and truly believe what I'm saying in the joke."

"I make fun of everyone, I'm not targeting anyone specific."

Each time I had an answer for why there was <u>not</u> a valid reason that these jokes were innocent. At this point I was a little shocked.

I said several times, "I'm not saying you're racist, I really don't care and I'm not going to tell you what to say, but the point is these jokes ARE racist in nature and you don't get to determine whether or not they are insensitive. You have to admit that." (Right? RIGHT?).

They could not concede this point and adamantly denied having anything against any sort of race. I really was dumbfounded.

By now Todd, the only sober one was getting upset and began attacking me a bit. I held my temper and told them several times, "We shouldn't talk about this; it's obvious no one is going to convince anyone of anything." I said I should just go because I was beginning to get uncomfortable from Todd's aggressiveness. He raised his voice even more and tried angrily to make a point.

I simply said, "Look, you're just mad," and he replied, "No, if I was mad, I would be kicking and punching you in the face."

I was astounded. It was clear he wouldn't actually take it to that level and that he was trying to exert some masculine/tough guy edge over me. I shook my head and stood up from where I was sitting on the floor. I started to grab my things and said aloud to the room, "This is ridiculous."

After I quickly gathered my belongings I opened the front door and stopped and turned to Todd. I told him, "You need to grow the fuck up" and left.

Ok then...

At the speed of light, an interaction between members of the same racial group catches fire because of interracial matters. Again, that is one of the effects of neo-diversity. Just because people look like you, doesn't mean they believe like you or will accept just anything you say.

****

Nowadays, there are even more complex interpersonal situations. Another one of the legacies of racism is the belief, the assumption, that you can tell someone's racial group membership just by looking at the person. Turns out, though, that in the age of neo-diversity just because a person looks like you does not mean you have correctly identified their racial or ethnic group membership. One female student wrote:

Last summer I would go to the pool almost every day after my summer classes/labs and do some homework or play in the sand volleyball court. Now since I went almost every day I managed to make a few acquaintances and since I used to play volleyball in high school I couldn't help but want to join the games. So every time I went to the pool I saw the same group of friends and we'd always team up to play volleyball against whoever wanted to play against us.

One day a group of guys who were of Arabic descent wanted to play against our group and so we started a friendly game of volleyball, or so I thought. Since they were Arabic and one of the guys said he was Muslim, the guys on my team started making jokes, calling them terrorist, and that maybe we should let them win because they might "blow us up."

At this point I couldn't take it anymore so I looked at one of the guys that was making most of the rude comments and I said "actually I'm Arabic ...AND Muslim." I don't think I will ever forget his face when I said that, or anyone else who was around for that matter. I felt a rush of adrenaline and anger.

This is not the first time I have received the look of pure astonishment when I tell people I'm Arabic or Muslim and I guess it's because I don't fit into the stereotype of what a Muslim person is "supposed" to look like. So the guy literally didn't believe me, he kept repeating "no you're not," "you can't be," and my favorite one, "how?" And all I could say was "yes I am."

He continued to ask me where I was from and that it was really cool that I could speak Arabic and that I "don't look Muslim at all." I could tell how guilty and uncomfortable he felt for doing that. So after the awkward conversation of him apologizing and again

71

repeating that it was really "cool" that I was Muslim, he left the game and I don't think I ever saw him at the pool again.

Talk about "BREAKING NEWS." *"Actually I'm Arabic ...AND Muslim."* It's tough out there. You see, that particular legacy of racism is pretty pervasive. American's have been taught to identify race and ethnicity by skin color. Well that really doesn't work in our now truly neo-diverse country. And so this particular kind of mistake is being made by a lot of people in America, and on the NCSU campus. Another female student wrote:

Okay, so I work on campus at a desk at one of the dorms. Working at the desk, I get to interact with ALL TYPES of people. This one particular day a couple of Black girls came to the desk. I knew one of them because she had also worked at the desk at one point. They didn't need anything; they just wanted to chat. Somehow we got on the topic of race. They started by explaining that they are mostly Black, but that they did have some Indian (Native American) lineage.

One girl then asked me, "What are you"?

I knew what she meant so I replied, "I am Jamaican and Indian. I am mixed with other things, but that is most of it."

I know that my appearance is a little ambiguous. Usually people cannot tell what I am, so I honestly do not mind if they ask.

In response she said "Jamaican??? You're not even dark skinned!"

This really bugs me, but I tried to respond calmly.

"Well not all Jamaicans are dark skinned... the same way that not all Black people look a certain way."

She then said "Well, do you smoke weed?"

At this point I was just disappointed in her.

So I bluntly replied, "Not all people that are from an island smoke weed."

I was really irritated at this point. I feel like many people automatically put me in this box as soon as they hear that I am Jamaican. And now this black girl was using every stereotype she could think of! After this she asked me if I considered myself Black- my response was yes (I embrace all of my identities. If she had asked me if I considered myself Indian I would have also said yes). This has always been something I was unsure of because for some strange reason many people (including this girl) I have encountered down south don't seem consider Jamaicans to be Black. She then asked me what kind of Indian I was. I explained to her that I am East Indian. I guess she didn't know what that meant because she said "Oh, you mean Native American- not those kind (pointing to the East Indians in the computer lab behind her), you know, the kind that stink."

I had no idea how I was supposed to respond to something as blatantly disrespectful as that! I wasn't sure if she was being rude because she honestly thought I was not "one of those kinds of Indians" so it was okay to talk that way around me or if she was too stupid to know that it was offensive. Even if I wasn't "one of those kinds of Indians" I would have still been appalled at the fact that she thought, for even a second, that her statement was appropriate.

I replied, "Actually, I am exactly that type of Indian- the kind that stinks! Is there anything else you would like to talk about?"

I could tell she was embarrassed. Her eyes widened, she stopped talking, and there was an awkward pause in the conversation. She apologized, but it didn't make me feel any better. I was pissed. I haven't ever looked at her the same. I would hope that she will grow up and learn about the world and different cultures, but I don't even understand where someone like her should even start.

I think it's just sad.

At the speed of light, another interaction has gone terribly wrong. Interacting with a person whose race is not easily identifiable fills some people with anxiety. Burning with anxiety and uncertainty, hoping to reduce the heat, Person A tries to quickly figure out what racial group Person B belongs to. It is as if Person A can't live in the inferno of not knowing "…what are you?" Working under the duress of the heat of their own anxiety, working hard, fast and psychologically sweaty to figure it out, the person with the need-to-know is barely listening to what's being said. Not listening, sweating from the heat of their own anxiety, making even more assumptions, other hot offensive stereotypes come flying out of Person A's mouth. *"Oh, you mean Native American- not those kind (pointing to the East Indians in the computer lab behind her), you know, the kind that stink."*

Those kinds of mistakes are being made and interpersonal interactions are catching fire. All that heat means it really is tough out there. Because of neo-diversity people are finding themselves in tough situations, having to make tough interpersonal decisions. One student wrote:

A few months ago I decided to go to a bar in Chapel Hill called "East End" with my fraternity brothers on a Tuesday night. Tuesday night's theme was "country night" because beers were $1 and country music continuously played all night long (until the bar closed), which was enticing considering the low *price of beers and a different atmosphere than the usual. On the way to Chapel Hill, I received a text from my best friend, Billy, who informed me that he would also be at country night with some friends of his and was excited that I was coming. My anxiety instantly rose because the thought of mixing Billy and his friends with my fraternity brothers would be challenging and probably threatening to our friendship.*

Now let me tell you about my friend. Billy is gay and an African American. He has been my friend for a few years now, sharing classes together and occasionally getting lunch/dinner when our schedules allowed the time. Billy also has a boyfriend who has recently become my friend too. Billy's helped me through tough situations with family and has always been there for me if I need him. Let's just say Billy and me are very close friends.

Now back to the story.

After receiving the text, the only thought that came to mind was, "Oh no." I knew that the situation would be tough and had to think of something to do to keep both Billy and my fraternity brothers separate from each other. We finally arrived and went into the bar. My brothers went to get a drink and I intensely searched for Billy to see if they were here yet. I spotted them at a booth in the corner of the bar. Hoping to prevent a possible interaction, I motioned to my brothers to sit at a table on the opposite side of where Billy was sitting.

My fraternity is very conservative and most of the members do not take interest in other guys who aren't Greek, republican, or not belonging to the Caucasian race. They use "gay" as meaning stupid, ridiculous, and irrational, etc. and also use the word to refer to homosexuality in a negative connotation. Given that

Billy was homosexual as well as African American, I knew that my brothers wouldn't be ok with him hanging around us. Trying to protect Billy from being hurt from slander comments or smirks from my brothers, I continuously "hid" or prevented myself from Billy finding me so he wouldn't come over and say hello. He saw me and walked over.

As he approached me with a hug, he said, "Hey Will! How have you been?"

I acted normal and hugged back asking how he was doing.

Billy said, "I'm great!"

Then Billy looked at my fraternity brothers and said, "What's up guys I'm Billy."

The brothers looked up at him with disgust and an antagonistic smirk as he introduced himself. One of them looked up and said, "Dude we aren't fags or like niggs...." Billy's smile quickly faded and looked up at me, expecting me to say something.

I was speechless.

Awkward silence.

Billy turned and began walking away as my fraternity brothers burst into laughter saying "What a dumbass, expecting us to befriend a homo?" I stood there in silence, feeling powerless, wishing I would have said something.

Here we have a very different kind of neo-diversity dilemma. In the face of intolerance, this young man gave in to conformity. That is something we social psychologists have studied since the 1940s. Conformity is giving in to perceived group pressure. And in this case he could feel the very real, very hot, group pressure to go along with intolerance. Yeah, he's your friend but we're your fraternity brothers and your friend is both "...a homo and a nigg..." In the face of that red hot intolerance, that young man made the classic mistake.

He did what too many do.

He panicked, gave in, and too late realized he had set himself on fire.

Chapter Five

Children of Light?

"The greatest tragedy of this age will not be the vitriolic words and deeds of the children of darkness, but the appalling silence of the children of light."
Martin Luther King, Jr.

As the semester begins to wind down, I introduce these words of Martin Luther King, Jr. Although Dr. King spoke those words in the 1960s, how well they apply to the neo-diversity of NCSU (and America). All of the groups I speak to on and off campus eventually admit to the problem of silence in the face of intolerance. Students at NCSU tell me that when other people use religious, ethnic, gender or racial slurs, it makes them uncomfortable. My students tell me that they know letting these words pass unchallenged is wrong, but they still let it pass. I ask why? You say you are uncomfortable. You say you don't approve. So why do you let it pass? In every audience I speak to, someone answers, "... you don't want to be the odd one out." So in the face of true intolerance, students give in to conformity pressures; they yield to perceived group pressure.

We let intolerance go unchallenged on our campus.

We show tolerance for intolerance.

"That's so gay!"

We give that intolerance permission to get louder and louder. Our silence creates a sound. And so our silence, our not speaking up, has a sound. A loud, screeching, hateful sound:

Fags... burn... Die!

On university property, on our Gay, Lesbian, Bi-sexual, Transgender Center, out of the darkness there came that sound at the top of the lungs of hate; a sound that was encouraged by silence in the face of intolerance. Who wants to live in a place where voices from the darkness loudly make the sound of hate? Who would claim to be from such a place?

"Oh...you go to school over there... that place that is so loud with hate?"

As the semester winds down, after students in the class have learned a lot of the social psychology of neo-diversity anxiety, tension, and hostility, I take up the tough topic; language. Language that is used against groups, language used to keep and maintain social distance and segregation: racial, gender, ethnic, religious slurs.

There are no innocent slurs. The point of using classic racial slurs is the same point for using all group slurs. These words are power words designed to put people in their place. No one can call an African American a nigger in a friendly way. No one, black, white, brown, yellow, can make that word, or any group slur, friendly.

Black people calling each other "...nigger" is just as unacceptable as whites or members of other groups doing so. That practice is unacceptable because it is done for the same reason: to make an interpersonal power move. Use of the word "...nigger" is always an attempt to say "I am superior to you." How so?

Some parts of our language have an intergroup character. Words are used to distinguish us versus them, and with that superior versus inferior. Not only that, the intergroup character of language has a history. Saying that "...I didn't mean it <u>that</u> way" means you know about that history. Turns out, that history is so strong you can't change the meaning of the word; there is no other way to use the word.

Jabara Asim writes with clarity about this in his book, "The N-Word." Mr. Asim writes: "…the word 'nigger' serves primarily—even in its contemporary 'friendlier' usage—as a linguistic extension of white supremacy, the most potent part of a language of oppression that has changed over time from overt to covert."

Going on, Asim says, "'Nigger'… is not one of those words of innocuous meaning that morphed over time into something different and harmful; *it has always been tethered to notions of race and racial inferiority.*"

So one African American saying to another, "What's up… my nigger," is not friendly or affectionate. It is one black person reminding another black person of their place in the racial hierarchy of America. "My nigger…" "You're nothing special, just another nigger." Not only that, but, "I can talk to you this way because I own you like a slave. You are after all, *my* nigger." Yes, coming from African Americans too that language rests on and perpetuates the legacy of racism.

To make that friendly, you have to do an impossible psychological dance. It's impossible because the minute a white person, a really good friend, an intimate says it, the music stops playing and all hell breaks loose. So in fact the word has only one hateful meaning. That's the social psychological lesson I teach. Group slurs are words of interpersonal power, designed to put a person "…in their place."

Hear the Wolfpack howl.

A black male student wrote:

The most intense interracial dyadic interaction that I have ever experienced happened rather recently. A new album had just released, my roommates and I were going over to a house of their friends in order to drink a few beers – we're all of age of course, and to listen to the Carter IV (Artist Lil' Wayne). I had never met three of the four guys whom all lived in the house we were going to, so I wasn't sure what to expect. As soon as my roommates and I open the door to the house the very first thing I hear is, "Hey niggers!" They had never met me so had no clue that I was a black male, nor had I ever met them and had no clue that they were all white males. At first I wasn't 100% sure that I had heard what I thought I had heard so I sort of looked to see if my roommates, who are both white males, had any sort of reaction because they were ahead of me and one was already in the house. One of my roommates claimed he had heard nothing, which wasn't possible because he was the one already inside the house – so I know if I heard it he had to have heard it since it was clearly audible. I had not driven to the house, and both of my roommates were excited to hear the album so I made light of the situation and continued into the house unsure and weary of how the night could potentially go – bad idea number one.

When we came into vision of the house mates and they noticed that I was black, they acted as if they had said nothing out of the ordinary. As countless thoughts raced through my head as to how I should handle the night, my palms became sweaty and I quickly had to figure out how to remove myself from the situation. The night progressed and we began to drink our beer – bad idea number two. As we sat in a small bedroom with black lights all around us, drinking, and the Carter IV shaking the very walls of the room, I look around and notice that most eyes are fixed upon me and I feel my heart began to race. In my head I was in hostile territory and needed to make damn sure I stood my ground. It was then I had the idea to text both of my roommates informing them that I felt it was a good time to leave. I spent nearly half an hour to forty-five minutes of trying to convince the driver that we should leave. At one point in the text message conversation he told me, "You can go sit on the couch outside" in response to my demands to remove ourselves from the situation.

The album finally comes to an end and I can escape this anxious situation. I immediately stand and suggest that we get home in order to catch the remainder of the Monday night football game. We eventually got in the car and on our car ride home we had a very intense conversation about how inappropriate it was for their friends to shout "Hey niggers!" I was infuriated and explained how in that type of situation it felt like it was me against them all, and I felt belittled. I was so frustrated and pissed off at the driver for thinking that the entire situation was okay and that I was making a big deal out of nothing, and even more for telling me that I should go sit on the couch outside! The conversation continued for nearly twenty minutes before we finally reached common ground.

You want to know what's trending? Whites calling each other nigger. Friendly or what? How innocent is that?

September 20, 2009, Dear Amy, a newspaper advice columnist received a letter in which a white writer was complaining about her white friends calling each other (and the white writer) "…niggas." Published in the Raleigh News & Observer, seeking advice about how to get her friends to stop this practice the writer wrote:

"I have a few white friends who throw the "N word" around with an "a" at the end. It makes me uncomfortable when

they use it, especially when they use it to describe me (I am white)."

Dear Amy answered by calling this practice unacceptable. Her answer was a good one, but I was puzzled.

My puzzlement had to do with why this group of white people got such apparent joy out of doing this. That quandary of mine grew when I got that paper you read earlier, from one of my students in which he described the same practice among his white acquaintances. He was uncomfortable and he was verbal in saying to his friends that their behavior was "...racist." Interestingly, his friends argued that they were just having fun; that this was harmless.

My puzzlement went nuclear when I got a paper from a white female who said it made her "angry" that blacks could call themselves "niggers" but she wasn't allowed to. Really, I wondered... it makes you angry? Why in the world would that be the case?

Keep in mind that when I teach about the use of racial and other anti-group slurs, I make the point that these slurs are used for one reason: to display power. The use of anti-group slurs is to pull the "...superiority card."

Whites who call each other nigger do so to show they are *still* superior to blacks. Since by being white the term cannot actually apply to them, they are just showing that they know that there are *still* niggers in the world. They are saying that they believe and enjoy the idea that there are *still* people who by their skin color are inferior to them. That's why those whites say that it's fun; we're just making fun *of them.*

As for those whites who say, "Well if they call each other that then why can't I call them that?" What an arrogant, transparent argument. Most whites who call each other niggers do not do so in the presence of black people. Not surprising because most know there would be negative consequences because those whites know there is only one way to use the word "...nigger," however it is spelled. Yet some whites want to be able to use the word. Why? There is only one possibility: to show that whites are *still* superior to blacks. Whites who do this are making a white supremacy claim. It is pulling the "...superiority card." Those whites seem to be saying "...because I am white, I have the right to use this word." Those whites seem to be saying, "Look, we invented the word to use against them, so it's our word after all." Indeed... that also explains why a young white person would become "...angry" because that white person can't call black people niggers, even though some black people call each other that.

Angry about what? How is not being able to call a black person or a white friend a nigger a detriment to your everyday life? What does it take away from you? Whatever your skin color, ethnicity or religion, answer me that.

One white female wrote:

Growing up in America, I have always felt that race-related tensions were centered around language. Different words used in and about different groups (primarily black and white) always felt like one of the biggest socially dividing forces. I felt like I couldn't say certain things to some people and expected they respect the same reservations in the way they spoke towards me. As it turns out, that feeling was based on language communities; a set of people in regular or symbolic interaction who assign unique meaning to words and symbols as a way of establishing and maintaining group membership and mutual understanding.

However, not all word use is the result of language communities. Racial slurs still bear no fair explanation. The misconception that the black race is raising itself together in unity by using the same words white people have confined them with for over a century is not only absurd but dangerous.

> *White people are just as guilty; when white groups use the word "nigger" to refer to one another, they are simply asserting their white superiority. It feels like blacks are being made the butt of a vulgar joke when white people use the word in a funny, insensitive manner. The truth is, [the word] has the ability of stirring up a year's worth of hateful feelings that we should be learning to excel past. While acknowledging the volatile racial history of the United States, we need to make the effort to grow from it.*
>
> *As a society, America has made great strides in the way it reacts to racial confusion. Instead of brushing aside race problems, they are, to an extent, studied and lamented upon. That just has not been enough though. When, as a society, will we learn the strength of these language communities and racial slurs?*

When indeed? But listen and hear that howl of this member of the Wolfpack. She wrote:

The misconception that the black race is raising itself together in unity by using the same words white people have confined them with for over a century is not only absurd but dangerous. White people are just as guilty. When white groups use the word "nigger" to refer to one another, they are simply asserting their white superiority. It feels like blacks are being made the butt of a vulgar joke when white people use the word in a funny, insensitive manner.

Some words have an intergroup history. Just because you weren't born during that history doesn't mean you can make words mean what you want them to mean. You can't change the history. Racial slurs were designed to be and continue to be used as interpersonal power words; to put people in their place.

Now the howl starts to become a chorus; a pack.
One white female student wrote:

In the New York City suburb of Westport, Connecticut racial and gender slurs were undoubtedly present. However, when I came to North Carolina State University for my freshman year of college, I started hearing slurs and terms that I didn't know existed. From this class I have learned that all slurs "...serve the function of a) describing a power relationship between two groups; these words describe a negative pattern of intergroup interdependence" (Nacoste).

Slurs have never seemed appropriate to me. As a child of two mothers, the term dyke offends me. As a human being the word N-gger boils my blood. I used to think they were just used because of ignorance or based on a person's upbringing. However, when I applied the motivation of power into past situations, everything made a little more sense.

For example, when I first heard my boyfriend say the n-word, he soon found out it would be the last time he was going to say it around me. From that point on he adjusted his vernacular, at first for me, and now to be respectful of all those around him (his words!). But then he got mugged. Five African American men pointed guns to his head and took his watch, hat, and the $300 he had been saving in his wallet. The first time we discussed the incident, he was nothing but upset and scared for his life.

Not too long after, we spoke again. By this time his anger had set in. The racial slurs were being said to no end! I didn't know what to do being caught in a whirlwind of his and my own emotions. After about five minutes of nonstop ranting, he came back down to earth and apologized to me, but now I understand the root of his behavior a little better.

Looking back, my boyfriend's rapid use of these words in that situation were all stemming from his lack of power. He had five gun barrels pointing at his head, no power or control in sight. He was saying the slurs to put himself in the power position by degrading the men that hurt him. The desire for control is a strong one especially in situations like this. However, the use of these words will not gain power for anyone. I think that this new idea can be a great asset in future intergroup interactions when these slurs are used. I can use it as a clear and well thought out reasoning for why these degrading terms should not be used.

You can't get around it. Nigger is a power word. Even when young women call each other bitches and sluts, these are interpersonal power words that are used to tell people to "…remember your place."

****

What should a person do in the face of another person's use of anti-group slurs? Should you call the person out by calling them names?

Racist!

Homophobe!

Sexist!

No; name calling is just name calling. Name calling is also a power move that is divisive. Well then, you ask, what should I do? One male student wrote:

The most important new thought that I now have is knowing the differences between prejudice, bigotry, and racism. Prejudice is an unfair, negative reaction to a group of people. Bigotry is the outward, behavioral expression of prejudice. Racism is always in the institutional structure of a society, it is never interpersonal. Racism supports prejudice and bigotry. Whenever I use to hear someone say something negative about someone of a different race, religion, or gender, racism was always the first thing to come to mind. But, as the definitions show, the person just holds a prejudice, and when they let it out, it becomes bigotry.

I see people different now. If I hear someone on the television or in person say something negative about an out-group, I don't automatically jump to the conclusion that they are racist. I now know that no one is innocent. We all have prejudice about an out-group, and we all have the potential to commit bigotry by letting one of those prejudices show in our behavior. Knowing this is going to change how I look at other people when their anxiety levels get high and they let one of their prejudices slip out.

Now when I am watching television with some friends and someone on it says something negative about an out-group, and one of my friends calls them a racist, I can correct them and explain what is really going on. Also, if I am ever talking with someone that is in an out-group from me and they say something negative about my in-group, although I will be upset and have to walk away, I will know that it is out of anxiety of being in an intergroup interaction and not out of pure racism. Also, if I am ever talking to a person of my in-group and they say something negative about an out-group, I will know that it is a prejudice coming out rather than racism. I will also now know how to handle the situation.

If I am ever in a situation where this occurs, I know that I don't tell the person that they are wrong or that it's not a good idea to talk that way. I just need to calmly express how it makes me feel uncomfortable and that it hurts me. This is letting the other person know that if they want to remain my friend, they have to refrain from speaking like that; at least in my presence. Also, speak for yourself, not for the other person; for example, say things like "I am uncomfortable," not things like "you are a racist."

I have learned so much useful stuff this semester in this class, but this is the one thing that has stood out to me the most through the whole semester. Although I have examples to go along with just about every topic we have covered this semester, this seems to be the one that seems to occur the most to me and my friends. This will be one topic that I will never forget.

I have a number of goals in my teaching "Interpersonal Relationships and Race." Yes, one goal is to raise student's knowledge and awareness of neo-diversity. My second goal, however, is to help students live well in the context of this unavoidable neo-diversity. That requires that I teach strategies for managing neo-diversity anxiety and the intolerance that anxiety can sometimes activate.

Remember, I have the long view. I started working on diversity issues in the U.S. Navy in 1974. Back then diversity was all about black-white relations. But diversity in black and white is dead. Neo-diversity is what we live with today; a time and circumstance when for all of us, contact with people who do not look like us happens every day, and is unavoidable. Many people are having trouble adjusting to our neo-diversity America. Not so much because of prejudice and bigotry, but because of uncertainty and anxiety about how to interact.

Today my work is about neo-diversity with mixed groups on and off our campus. From college students, middle school students, to people over 50, I have learned that one of the biggest neo-diversity problems in America is that moment when someone in a group utters words of intolerance. In all of the groups I teach and work with, that moment is described with this reaction: "I am very uncomfortable when people do this, but I don't know what to do. So I don't say or do anything."

Silence, it turns out, is a bad idea. Silence lets stereotypes live on. Silence gives power to racial slurs, slurs against our gay, lesbian and transgendered brothers and sisters, and slurs against our Muslim brothers and sisters. Silence gives power to division. When we are silent in those moments, we show too much tolerance for intolerance. That's why we end up with all kinds of racial and hateful graffiti.

When we are silent we let people go on automatic. Not to put too fine a point on it, but silence lets people go on automatic, never having to consider the ugly, hurtful and divisive impact of their words or the images they send around. In clear evidence of this is the 2011 episode in which President Obama was depicted as a chimpanzee in an email distributed by an elected representative of the Orange County (California) Republican Central Committee. People all over the country were outraged because of the historical, demeaning practice of referring to black people as monkeys.

In her written apology, Ms. Marilyn Davenport said, "I didn't stop to think about the historic implications and other examples of how this could be offensive..." "*I didn't stop to think...*" is the most important part of her statement. No excuse, but that reflects the too often experienced social reality. Some Americans get in their in-groups and talk negatively about other Americans in group terms without ever being challenged about that way of talking. So, when in another social context having gone unchallenged before, those people go on automatic and we get pictures of the President of the United States depicted in racially offensive ways.

Will we ever stop that intolerance completely? No. Can we, you and I, influence how often it happens? Yes. But the change we want will not come through text messaging, Facebook or tweets. The change we want will come from what we do in our face-to-face social interactions and relationships.

Each of you has the power to influence your social interactions. When the person you are interacting with uses negative racial, gender or ethnic language, do not tolerate it. But don't call that person names, like racist, sexist, homophobe. Instead of name-calling, speak for yourself.

Don't try to tell that person they are wrong. Don't try to tell that person it's just not a good idea to talk that way.

Here's the interpersonal strategy. Let that person know your standards for continuing to interact with you. Just quietly, but firmly, express your personal standard for the interaction. Speak into that moment, and speak for yourself. Simply say, "I am very uncomfortable with that kind of language. I find it offensive. It hurts me." If the person persists, walk away from the interaction. It's time for all of us to wake up and take personal responsibility for what goes on in our interactions with other people.

Especially the first time you do it, I understand that this will not be easy. Even as you begin to make your statement, you will feel the conformity pressure. And you will want to give in to that pressure. That funny feeling in your stomach will make you want to just let it pass. But here's the thing. Your silence will be taken as approval. That means that every time you interact with Person A, that person will assume you are OK with anti-group slurs and language. You will have to live with that hateful language in your interactions with Person A. Is that what you want? Can you do that?

Instead, use your interpersonal power in the moment. Using your inside voice just say "...I am very uncomfortable with that kind of language. I find it offensive. It hurts me." And again, if the person persists, walk away from the interaction.

It is a quiet but effective strategy. This is not my personal opinion. I teach this as a social psychologist, a scholar of intergroup relations and a research scientist. And the experimental research[7] shows that kind of statement makes a difference. The results of the research tell us two things. One, that quiet statement reduces the other person's tendency to ever talk using stereotypes or to use slurs against groups. Two, that quiet statement also makes the person feel bad about their intolerant words. Believe me, the more of us who with soft but clear voices stand up to intolerance, the less people around us will be likely to go on automatic and verbalize their intolerance.

If we really want change, silence is no longer an option. When we are silent we give power to the idea that speaking in stereotypes and slurs is OK. That is why history repeats itself. But now is our opportunity to begin to change that. You see, it is in the small interaction moments where the next big change will occur. Now is your opportunity to create change in the small moments.

After teaching this, I have seen the light go on in my student's eyes. Now they have a way, a strategy, to stand up to intolerance in their everyday, social lives. That gives students' power. One white female student wrote:

> *Throughout my life I have been surrounded by terribly negative words like bitch, nigger, and faggot from the likes of the media, rap music, my schooling and even my grandfather. I always knew these words were wrong and hurtful to others but they were used so*

---

[7] Czopp, A. M., Monteith, M.J. & Mark, A. Y. (2006). Standing up for change: Reducing bias through interpersonal confrontation. Journal of Personality and Social Psychology, 90 (2006): 784-803.

frequently and in a playful manner that their true meanings were gradually downplayed.

While I wish I could say differently, because I did know better, I confess I often took part in using these words. Reflecting now on my past, I can see that I made a choice to use those vile words in order to seem "normal." In fact, the use of these words was and is normal but I have grown to find that the use of these words can be very dangerous.

I, being a huge supporter of the GLBT community, am ashamed to know that I ever allowed myself to utter the words "fag," "homo" or "that's so gay." Now when I hear such hateful speech, I do not join in, in fact I make a point to let a person know they are offending me when they use such words or phrases. One thing I like to point out to people is how odd it is that "that's straight" is used to describe something as being cool or good whereas "that's gay" is always a completely negative phrase.

I believe many times it is these silent decisions to use such language that keeps this language so prevalent. Many people, I am sure, are now numbed to these words and thus, use them in their daily vocabulary. The danger of these words was displayed just months ago when many teens took their lives after being publicly ridiculed and harassed for being openly gay. Stories like these tear at my soul and I hope others have learned from these suicides that words are powerful.

I have come to understand the power of words, especially negative words such as bitch, slut, nigger, and faggot. Though I too once participated in throwing these words around I now know why. I made a silent choice. In the future I hope to turn others way from making that same choice. Informing another person that their words are offensive to us gives them a negative stimulus to attach to that word and hopefully they will reassess their use of such hateful terms. I will not put up with these horrific words and one day I hope to work with the Human Right Campaign (or various other organizations) to solve problems like these. Though I have begun to speak out against their use because they are offensive to me, I cannot do it on my own. These words are nothing but terribly, tragically, unfortunately, hateful terms and I will not be silent.

She says, "I cannot do it on my own."
She needn't have worried.
Hear the echoing howl from the Wolfpack.
Another student wrote:

"The greatest tragedy of this age is not the vitriolic words and deeds of the children of darkness, but the appalling silence of the children of light." Dr. Nacoste ended the lecture that day, November 16, with those powerful words of Dr. Martin Luther King Jr. with such strength, with such intensity that I could feel chills move from shoulder to hands, and a hard knot in my throat as my nose tingled with emotion. I fully realized at that moment that there was no turning back.

"Waiting on the world to change" as John Mayer put it simply was not going to work for me anymore. The semester was full of lessons that I wasn't ready for, but sometimes those are the best ways they are learned. I am not innocent. I was introduced and read one of the most influential books I have read, "Blood Done Sign My Name." From that book and Dr. Nacoste's lectures I have seen myself change in ways I never thought I would, mainly because I didn't think I needed to change really.

The most influential change from this course is I have realized that I can no longer go about my life, encouraging demeaning group language, offensive jokes, slurs, and so on by being silent. In situations when necessary, and using the right tools, I need to become the opinion deviant, meaning I deviate from the in-group norm (language). In a group setting, where this happens I don't have to stand around waiting for something to change, there is a strategy for being an opinion deviant and coming out of the group when offensive stereotypes are made.

Many of my friends from high school and now in college still partake in these "jokes" using race, ethnicity, gender, religion all as the punch line. Before, I was never comfortable enough to use these jokes, because somewhere in me I knew that although they were being used for "humor," those subjects just aren't something that should be joked about. However I cannot count the number of times I have heard these jokes, "Why are women's feet so small? So they can stand closer to the oven," or slurs, or "What up my nig," or stereotypes, "Well of course she got an A on the math test, she's Asian" and stayed silent.

Stayed silent out of not wanting to be the odd one out, that may be put out of the group by voicing an opinion. And until this course I never realized how to do this in a manner with which I would be comfortable in. Granted I know the first few times I try this it will feel funny, but I feel like at least now I have a game plan.

First off, by not making the statement accusatory, but a statement of honest self-disclosure. Such as, "I would prefer that you don't use that kind of language around me," "I really don't like it that you say such racially offensive stuff," and "I really don't like that you refer to people in stereotypes." These statements seemed intimidating at first but actual social psychological research shows that confrontations like those are effective in the immediate situation, and causes the person using a slur to experience negative self-evaluations. Also in any social interaction managing interpersonal conflict is necessary, and if the other person cannot respect my values, then in the end they should not be someone that I have a real relationship with.

I am done waiting, being scared for our generation in this chaotic time where the beast of neo-diversity reigns. I am ready to be a part of a quiet revolution.

That is the howl of the Wolfpack.

****

My students find having a strategy empowering because they have stumbled against and been confused by neo-diversity. With a new awareness, with a strategy in hand using the words of Martin Luther King, Jr., my students start to call themselves "children of light" who are ready to be part of a quiet revolution. One student wrote:

The fact that we now live in a society defined by neo-diversity that produces anxiety, it is no wonder, and very clear, that there are no innocent. Not you, not me. The fact that we are all humans, interacting in social situations largely contributes to our lack of innocence. No matter how much we try to be fair, just, and accepting, our initial thoughts and instincts may be less than worthy or acceptable. Now that we are children of light, we must conquer the silence, be aware of the world around us, and strive to educate others while simultaneously promoting and exemplifying justice to all.

Another wrote:

The anxiety about interacting with other races in our personal life is at an all time high in America. To understand how to adjust and comfortably interact with other races we first have to understand that every individual in America has this anxiety. As Dr. Nacoste presented to class "Life comes at you fast, don't panic." The neo-diversity effect can create anxiety which can lead to panic, so take a break; calm down. Anxiety can lead to nothing positive and more than likely will make you end up eating your words as soon as you begin this interracial interaction. Practice makes perfect, get out there and talk to other races, ethnicities, learn about other people's culture. If everyone can take this step we as a whole can begin our "QUIET REVOLUTION."

Yet even with a strategy, it will be tough out there. Have no doubt that there will still be social psychological forces to be dealt with. Forces that can be activated just by how a person looks will still be at work. With no thought, the color of another person's skin can cause anyone to automatically put people into us-versus-them categories. What do we do about that? One white male student wrote:

Throughout this course I feel that I have learned to appreciate the process of interaction between myself and those around me. There are many factors which influence those interactions as well and having a fuller understanding of those factors allows me to avoid pitfalls while interacting. The minimal group effect, or the automatic categorization of a person as either inside or outside of our group with a tendency to compete, draws attention to the way I initially perceive someone I meet and how I might see them as either inside or outside my group. With this in mind I could avoid competition with others by realizing our commonality instead of focusing on our difference which might make them outside my in-group.

Earlier last semester I had been assigned to live with a random roommate who I had never met named Chris. I shook his hand and told him it was nice to meet him and complimented his computer for some odd reason. During our first interaction I could sense our interaction anxiety due to our lack of knowledge as to how we should interact. He was a lighter skinned African American from what I could tell. He had roomed with our other suitemates, all of who are African American, over the summer and knew them well. I felt a little out of the loop and uneasy because of their already established friendships and the fact that I was the only white guy in the suite.

I recall one morning they were all in the hall talking while I was in bed, asleep to their knowledge. One noted jokingly about how the day before I had walked by and said, "What's up?" to him which was very funny for some reason. Chris said that he found me "very awkward" and wished he had his old roommate instead. This was very disheartening to me but I never confronted them about it. Later Chris came back to the room and noticed I was reading anime, a type of Japanese comic book, and immediately asked me about it and what my favorite one was and such. This interaction went much smoother than the others and I didn't feel nervous. He had found something in common with me and we were able to bond over it. We were no longer in out groups from each other and this allowed our friendship to grow.

I feel like this story shows how perceiving someone as either in or out-group can influence how you interact. Before this course I felt like my interactions with someone of another race were always hindered by the fact that I would perceive our difference in appearance as different groups from each other. I believe now that I should over look that to find ways in which we are similar and that will help me function better in my relationships with other races.

Yes, it will still be tough out there; tough but manageable. A white male student wrote:

Anxiety stemming from contact with out-group members. This is the way Dr. Rupert Nacoste defines the term Inter-Group Anxiety. But to truly grasp this concept, one must understand how this anxiety relates to social interaction. When a person is experiencing this inter-group anxiety it means they are feeling nervous when talking to people who are not in their in-group. This includes people of different genders, race, ethnicities, religions, social backgrounds, etc., etc., the list goes on and on. In fact some would argue that the list is getting longer and longer. The amount of interracial couples is on the rise, and many homosexuals are "coming out of the closet" so to speak as they now have less reason to fear rejection from the rest of society. This apparent increase in diversity, this neo-diversity, is without a doubt a positive change, as people should be able to be who they are without having to fear social rejection for being "different."

At the same time this neo-diversity is causing social confusion and uncertainty; no doubt a result of intergroup anxiety. People experience this when they come in contact with people who have different group identifications. For example if a white, heterosexual Christian comes in contact with a Hispanic, homosexual Buddhist, the two people are experiencing intergroup contact by means of race, sexuality, and religion. This creates an aspect of uncertainty as there are no rules and norms for such an interaction. Many people are afraid of seeming prejudiced towards the other person's group identification(s) and as a result try a little too hard to be friendly and polite. This will usually show in a person's facial expression and body language and create a strained conversation.

On the flip side some people will carry their personal prejudices into the interaction and not worry about whether or not those prejudices are obvious to the other person. In this scenario the person likely believes the stereotypes he or she has about the other person's group identification is correct so the person acts somewhat hostile in the interaction and tries to speed through it, in order "to just get it over with." From a logical standpoint, this just seems ridiculous. We all have differences even within our so called in-groups. Some of us are sports fans, some are not. Some are in to math, some are in to politics. People are different in many ways yet we allow certain differences to drive us apart, while others seem to not be such a big deal. But, we all do this. Inter-group anxiety is not something that only racist, stuck-up, holier-than-thou CEO's experience.

Somehow, some way, everyone has a misconception about a different race, religion, etc. and carries that into a relationship with a person of that particular out-group. People can do this without even realizing it, and when they start to feel nervous about talking to a member of an out-group their anxiety pushes those misconceptions to the surface. Once they come out the person will find him or herself backpedaling like they ran head first into a mob of French Revolutionaries. But this scary situation can be avoided. By making no assumptions, and just being yourself, intergroup anxiety will surrender to you and you can enjoy the interaction and possibly make a new friend.

The first step in doing this, however, is often the hardest step to overcome, because you have to first come to terms with the stereotypes you hold towards different out-groups. Once this is done, you can learn to get past these stereotypes so when you meet members of an out-group you can get to know them for who they really are, rather than putting a label on them and pushing them away. The final step is to ignore concerns about being rejected from your own in-group. This is the part of intergroup anxiety that many people lack the bravado to overcome. Rejection from a person's own in-group is sometimes the ultimate fear, and risking the safety of in-group friendships can be psychologically terrifying. But, only when this step is passed can a person begin to know people as people, and not as a black person, or as a bisexual person, or as a Muslim.

Once this is done the spell of non-law bound segregation can be broken, and people from all kinds of backgrounds can feel welcome among others, regardless of the region of the world they are living in. But this all starts with us as individuals. We have to learn to overcome our own inter-group anxiety in order to create a better world. As for me? I've learned to get past racial stereotypes, talk to a Muslim the same way I would talk to a Christian, and talk to a homeless person asking for change the same way I talk to my economics professor. And more importantly I no longer feel the least bit nervous about interactions with so called "out-group members," I know who I am and I know I can develop friendships across racial, religious, and any other social barriers.

Besides, once you learn the psychology behind it you realize, in-groups are for the weak-minded.

I know, and my students begin to believe that the effort is worth it. Not only worth it now, but the effort is worth it for our futures. A white female student wrote:

The funny thing about this course is that I've learned a pivotal thing about myself but not in the way I expected to. When you asked us to write about the most intense racial interaction we've ever had, I searched and I pondered and I searched some more and pondered some more. I thought to myself, "You're not reaching far enough! There is something you're not remembering." Then it hit me. I was at a loss for this assignment because I had not ever had a memorably intense racial interaction.

This was a crude wake up call for me. Here I am, someone who is a champion for racial equality and an addict of books on racial experiences and I had never encountered an intense racial moment. This was not because I'm simply an easy going person. This is because I've never put myself in that situation because I have one black friend I would consider a real friend and have not been exposed to anything else.

Even at a school of 35,000, I can't say I've made an effort. It's strange to me that this is the case. If someone says the 'N-word' it affects me to the core and changes my opinion of the user. This doesn't affect me personally; I don't have close black friends to protect.

Then I realized something.

I want interaction. I want friends with diverse cultures and backgrounds. Why else would I surround myself with literature and classes like this one if I didn't desire more relationships?

This is why I feel protective, and offended, when racial slurs are used. I'm protecting my desired future friends- something that I'm now going to work on. After all, from this class I have garnered all the tools to embark on more interpersonal relationships.

Ah the future…

Sometimes we forget that we are always building a future for ourselves. Sometimes we forget that we are always building a future for our children and for our nation. A white male student wrote:

I grew up in rural eastern North Carolina. In my hometown whites mostly isolated themselves from socialization with other ethnic and racial groups. I have observed that many of my peers from my hometown have been conditioned to only associate with other white people and they have developed racial tastes and preferences for primarily whites. I believe that they will continue to lead a life centered on whites in adulthood. They do not even recognize that their own racial segregation is an issue. They live their lives in ignorance just as if they were still adolescents. They have yet to experience a life enriched with other group cultures. My one new thought is that this is the fundamental problem with bigotry in youth in America. This thought has also provoked several ideas that involve my own future children and how I want to motivate them to seek out interracial friendships.

I believe I am unlike many of my peers from my hometown. I met an Indian boy while in high school and we have since become best friends. During the evolution of our relationship, I have noticed that I interact with Indian people on a more interpersonal level than before. I do not feel the mild social anxiety that I feel while interacting with some other ethnic groups and races. The relationship with my Indian friend has prepared me to engage in real interracial encounters with his group, and therefore leads to a reduction in my prejudice towards that group and other groups as well. Essentially, our friendship has reduced the intergroup tensions and uncertainties in my interactions.

If white youth are currently attending schools (both private and public) that are economically advantaged yet devoid of ethnic and racial diversity, then this is setting the stage for that youth's adulthood to be centered on people of their own race. This pattern could potentially sustain the ideology of white supremacy and the "us" versus "them" attitude. There needs to be a mix of groups so that the challenges of interpersonal conflict among interracial relationships can learn to be managed properly. The constant interactions with other groups should become a normal routine and this will help eliminate our youth's social anxiety.

This new thinking will help me function better in interracial encounters and relationships. I will not be hesitant to interact with individuals of other races or be reluctant to become friends with someone because of their ethnic group. I know that I need to involve myself in relations with other groups so that I will obtain the

105

skills needed to maintain healthy relationships with a variety of people.

More importantly, I am inspired to help my own future children associate themselves with other ethnic groups and races in order to reduce the gap of acceptance. I will provide them an understanding of the importance of a socially diverse lifestyle so that they too live happily in the social world, and ideally, they will spread this kind of understanding to their own peers and children.

Also about our future, a black female student wrote:

This class has by far been one of the most interesting classes I've taken thus far at NC State. It was very difficult for me to single out just one concept from this course to write about because we have covered so much. However, I think the one concept that stood out the most for me was the Neo-Diversity Effect. Neo-Diversity is defined as a new social uncertainty brought about by ongoing, rapid and substantive social changes. This Neo-Diversity produces a feeling of anxiety. This anxiety is the social uncertainty and in interracial or intergroup encounters, outcomes are not clear, or are ill defined, which makes the interaction unpredictable.

There are thousands of students on this campus of all different backgrounds, races and ethnicities. We meet new people and have countless interactions every day. While interacting with my peers of any race, I find that we share a common ideology. We are all State Students. We are all part of the Pack Nation. Everyone on campus knows the Wolf Sign. Everyone knows the School Song. Everyone cheers for the Power Sound of the South. We all bleed Wolfpack Red.

But there are times when that common ideology is not at the forefronts of our minds. When racially charged incidents occur on campus, they provide a stark color line across the bricks. When slurs again Middle Easterners of Arabic ethnicity are written in the Free Expression Tunnel, when we pass KKK members in the Brickyard, or when Hoodies are worn in silent protest, we no longer think as a singular unit, but are divided because of our perception of group inclusion. Who are the "we" and who among the "they?"

I guess we all see the division. It's not something that we can deny when these things happen. We all feel the anxiety, but I don't think anyone has ever recognized it for what it is. So after President Obama was elected, having a conversation with a person of a different race was like cutting through a jungle of tension. A normal chat becomes a guessing game. A white person assumes a Black person voted for him; a black person trying to determine if a white person voted for him. Neither knows the true answer, but the mere color of skin leads to assumption of beliefs. I don't believe that these assumptions will change overnight.

So my one new thought is this: awareness of Neo-Diversity will not change the actions of those who reproduce hatred. But it will change the way that we handle the incidents that separate us. We do not have to be separate. We do not have to hold ourselves captive to silence. We all feel the tension. Teaching others about Neo-Diversity doesn't relieve the tension, but it explains where it comes from. Even a little knowledge can change things in the hands of the right people. Spreading this knowledge will help us to function more smoothly in society because it will allow us to change our way of thinking.

Now that we know what separates us, we can make a choice. We can't get rid of it, but we can work around it. Color is not invisible. We cannot erase it. We cannot pretend it isn't there. But what we can do is remember the unity, remember the common ideology we have as a people. We are a nation made up of many different groups. But we are still <u>one</u> nation. Thinking differently can cause us to react differently. That's why understanding Neo-Diversity is so important.

We can be different and still be the same.

Why not be the "we" while still among the "they?"

All of you have the potential to be "…children of light."
Wolfpack! Who are you going to be?
What are you prepared to do?

Chapter Six:

The Strength of Neo-Diversity

Interpersonal relationships and race.

More than the fact that I am an interpersonal-social psychologist, the reason for my intense focus on the interpersonal in neo-diversity is that interacting with each other remains our great racial, ethnic, gender, religious, challenge. Have no doubt, fast and dramatic social changes have put us in the same situation as Dr. Seuss' Sneetches[8].

We rid ourselves of the immoral laws of racial segregation. With that and other changes in the social world, we are no longer able to say "…well they can't come in here. They can't come to our frankfurter parties." With that, some feel like Dr. Seuss' Starbelly Sneetches did:

> *"Good grief!"groaned the ones who had stars at the first…*
> *"We're **still** the best Sneetches and they are the worst.*
> *But, now, how in the world will we know," they all frowned,*
> *"If which kind is what, or the other way round?"*

Caught off guard by the changes, we struggle with neo-diversity anxiety in our interpersonal interactions. Even as

---

[8] Dr. Seuss (1961). <u>The Sneetches and other stories</u>. New York: Random House (p. 13; p. 21)

America becomes more and more diverse, nobody is telling citizens what that means. And so Americans, students at NCSU, are struggling with how to manage their day–to-day interpersonal lives because the old racial, gender, ethnic rules do not apply. Without laws and social understandings prohibiting who can go where, we all find ourselves interacting with people from other American racial, ethnic, gender and religious groups. We struggle then with the question, "who are among the 'we' and who are among the 'they?'" We are all Sneetches wondering:

*"Whether this one was that one… or that one was this one
Or which one was what one… or what one was who."*

With that neo-diversity anxiety we interact with people who do not look like or sometimes even sound like us. Our struggles today are intergroup struggles of interacting with many different American groups. Those interactions are formal and informal; at work, running errands, going to a sports bar, sitting in a classroom. In whatever social setting you find yourself, those interaction struggles are interpersonal.

****

Listen up, Wolfpack. My time is coming to an end. I have been at this work a long time. Indeed, I do have the long view. On the faculty at NCSU since 1988, I have been teaching about neo-diversity since 2006. And as you have read, my students learn that for change to happen, they have to work at it; they cannot sit around waiting… "waiting on the world to change."

Now you have a better sense of what's really going on: neo-diversity. And now you have a better sense of what is at stake, and what you might want to work on to make our campus one that you can be proud of because it is a place that accepts and celebrates all of its student-citizens, respecting the whole Wolfpack.

Tolerance is not enough. "We have to be more tolerant," is a weak interpersonal goal and strategy. Turns out that tolerance is the strategy of those who are worried, uncertain and anxious not those who are determined.

Tolerance is a poor strategy because tolerance is just "...putting up with" people. But we all know that putting up with someone is a strain. Putting up with someone makes you irritable, a little bit irrational, and so it makes the interaction unpredictable. When you are putting up with someone, even you don't know what you are going to say next. You can't get to acceptance if you are worried, uncertain, anxious and just putting up with the interpersonal moment until it is over.

A white female student wrote:

> *The fact that it is tough out there is the reason that I would like to focus this paper on the realization of the importance of our society acknowledging, understanding, and properly dealing with neo-diversity. I think that first and foremost we need to get rid of terms such as 'color-blindness' and 'post-racial' because they simply only serve to hinder our progress by allowing us to lie to ourselves and to ignore important underlying issues that have yet to be dealt with. People believe that we are in an age of color-blindness, however that ignorance is so far away from the truth. This false belief is a result of the fact that tolerance is confused with acceptance. These two terms not only mean different things they also have very different implications. Misinterpreting someone's tolerance for acceptance can get one into a world of trouble, because while you're thinking that someone is interacting with you because they accept you they may really just be doing it because they have to or feel obliged to.*

We need to realize that neo-diversity is not going anywhere; in fact, it is getting worse and worse as there are so many more so called out-groups out there than our own. I fear that people will lash out against these out-groups as time passes on, out of fear that their own identity and in-groups are being challenged or threatened in some way. I believe in the coming years that many people will show their true colors, and what I mean by this is that many people who were once thought of as accepting will reveal that they were only tolerating out-group members.

"*We need to realize that neo-diversity is not going anywhere,*" she wrote. True that, as some of you young people would say. How is it true?

In America today, intergroup contact is equal status. Every student on our campus is equally a member of the Wolfpack. By group, no one is better than the other. By group, no one is lower or higher than the other. Indeed, in America we no longer live in a society where our racial contacts are controlled and restricted by law. So it is no longer possible to avoid intergroup contact. It is no longer possible to control intergroup contact. Nowadays, every day, each of us has some occasion to interact with a person of another gender, religious, racial, ethnic, group. Today, then, our interpersonal encounters with individuals from other groups are not black and white but neo-diverse.

To live well within this neo-diversity, we have to move from tolerance to acceptance. It is at the interpersonal level that we live, and it is the interpersonal level of life that remains for us to work on. Our work now is to learn how to interact with each other, no matter the outward group membership of the other person. We can't afford to be Sneetches.

We need interpersonal leaders. An interpersonal leader is a person who stands up to conformity pressures in their everyday social interactions. We need people who will not be silent when anti-group slurs and stereotypes are used in conversation. We need people who will work to create and maintain a community of acceptance. We need people who will not only talk about new norms, but who with their behavior will set and display new interaction norms. To move from tolerance to acceptance... respect for all of the Wolfpack, we need people who will stand up for change.

After the November 2011, racial graffiti appeared in the Free Expression Tunnel, after all the public outcry and appropriate indignation, something went unnoticed, or at least unreported. But an African American female student wrote about what she saw on our campus:

> *The most important feature of America is that life is not all black and white. As far as my understanding, it appeared that interracial relations in the 60s were mostly between African-Americans and Caucasians. But after the brave few in society decided to break the color line, there was now a gray area; and this is where Neo-diversity first began. Neo-diversity is the new social uncertainty brought about by the rapid and substantive changes in the spheres of communication-technology, gender-relations, race and ethnicity, and international relations.*
>
> *In a cultural anthropology class, the teacher gave a group assignment where we were to go to 3 public places on campus and watch the activity of students and see if students automatically formed inter-groups. So the hypothesis was that despite the diversity of the campus, Blacks will associate with Blacks, Whites will associate with Whites, Indians will associate with Indians, etc. But my report was much different from that assumption. I went to the Atrium and observed a group of sorority girls, white, black, mixed, and Middle Eastern. It was actually a women's Engineering*

sorority. The common interest of the group wasn't skin tint, walks of life, or economic background. Even though there were white women in the group, they were the minority because they were female Engineers. Neo-diversity was at its best.

A more recent event that displayed Neo-diversity was the derogatory picture in the Free Expression Tunnel. Students planned to get together and paint the Free Expression Tunnel where they were able to voice their views against racism on NC State campus. But I can tell you what was expected. People expected a large group of pissed off African American students. Yet, once again against the norm, students of all ethnicities came to support the cause and paint the tunnel. Neo-diversity was at its strongest.

Students in those neo-diverse groups were interpersonal leaders. And because those students refused to be Sneetches, they experienced and showed the strength of neo-diversity. That is the real hope for more change at NCSU. The Wolfpack is that strong.

You see, wolves ban together to nurture and protect each other. Sometimes though, wolves get separated from each other. When wolves howl it is to call for the pack to come back together; to reunite.

Have you been listening? Did you hear in these NCSU student voices the howl of the Wolf? Did you hear the call for the pack to come together to accept and draw strength from its neo-diversity? That is a howl calling our pack to a new psychological location so that there we can stand with each other not wondering but knowing that <u>all</u> in the Wolfpack are the "…we."

Hear the howl.

Will you unite with the real Wolfpack?

What say you?

Afterword

"I was just thinking that of all the trails in this life there is one that matters most. It is the trail of a true human being. I think you are on this trail and it is good to see."

Dances With Wolves (1990)

Acknowledgements

My heartfelt thanks go out to the students who have taken my "Interpersonal Relationships and Race" course since 2006. Each of you knows that being and staying in that course required that you come face to face with some unsettling part of your interpersonal history. I thank you for sticking it out and growing from the experience. I thank you also for your stories, and for your permission to use your stories and your story-essays. Thank you for coming along with me on this trail toward our full humanity.

For editing I turned to Mr. Gideon Brookins. I have watched Gideon grow up into the strong, responsible young man he has become. That growth now includes his North Carolina State University degree in technical writing. Thanks Gideon for editing and improving this book.

Ms. Logan Collins was a student in the class the very first time I taught "Interpersonal Relationships and Race." Since graduating from NCSU Logan has become a dear friend to me. I am thankful for her continuing friendship. Right now, I thank her for reading the first draft of this book; thank you Logan for your insightful and helpful comments that made this a better book.

About the author

Dr. Rupert W. Nacoste is Alumni Distinguished Undergradute Professor of Psychology at North Carolina State University. After serving in and being honorably discharged from the U.S. Navy (1972-1976), Dr. Nacoste received his B.A. degree in Psychology from the University of Florida (1978), and his Ph.D. in Social Psychology from the University of North Carolina at Chapel Hill (1982). Beginning during his service in the Navy, for the last thirty-eight years Dr. Nacoste has worked on diversity issues as a facilitator of racial discussions and as a scholar of interpersonal and intergroup relationships.

A native of Opelousas, LA, a Louisiana black-Creole, Dr. Nacoste is always on the hunt for a bowl of good gumbo. When that search fails, he makes his own. No surprise, then, that the title of his published memoir is "Making Gumbo in the University" (2010; Plain View Press: Austin, TX).